"The talent of an artist is a gift to the world. When I started to collect, my eyes were my main capital. My eyes were the gift of God. A painter does not paint a picture for only one man's eyes. My heritage as a collector is to share and I can only return God's gift by making it possible for more than one man to see and understand the artist's talent".

Baron Hans Heinrich Thyssen-Bornemisza de Kaszon, 1983

All rights reserved. No part of this publication maybe reproduced, stored in a retrieval system, or trasmitted, in any form or by any means, electronic, machanical, photocopying, recording or otherwise, without prior written permission from the Fundación Colección Thyssen-Bornemisza.

© Publication. Fundación Colección Thyssen-Bornemisza, 1994.
© Photographs. Fundación Colección Thyssen-Bornemisza, 1994.
© Photographs: p. 33, 54, 103, 113, 117 (A. 883), 122, 127 (A. 852) and 137, The Thyssen-Bornemisza Collection, 1994.
© of the work:
    © Sucesión Joan Miró 1994
    © Visual E.G.A.P., Madrid 1994, of authorised reproduction.

I.S.B.N.: 84-88474-09-1
Depósito Legal: B-8032-1993

Preparation and production: LUNWERG EDITORES S.A.
Beethoven, 12 - 08021 Barcelona. Phone: (93) 2015933. Fax: (93) 2011587
Manuel Silvela, 12 - 28010 Madrid. Phone: (91) 5930058. Fax: (91) 5930070

Printed in Spain

Layout of book and cover design: Daniel Gil

GUIDE OF THE THYSSEN BORNEMISZA MUSEUM

TOMÀS LLORENS
MARÍA DEL MAR BOROBIA
CONCHA VELA

Contents

SECOND FLOOR

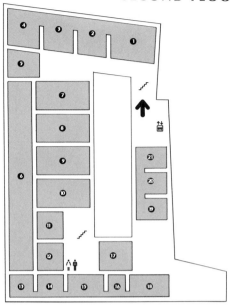

FIRST FLOOR

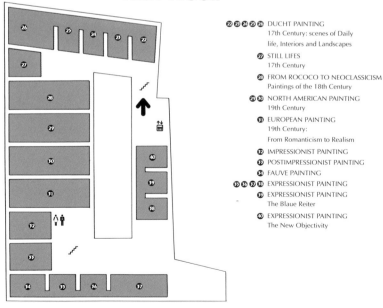

GROUND FLOOR

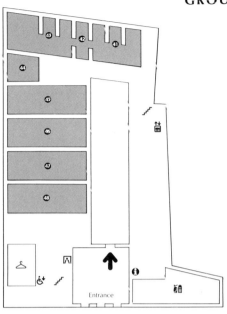

41 42 THE EXPERIMENTAL AVANT-GARDES
Paintings

43 GEOMETRICAL ABSTRACTION

44 ESSENTIAL CUBISM

45 THE SYNTHESIS
OF MODERNISM
Europe

46 THE SYNTHESIS
OF MODERNISM
U.S

47 48 SURREALISM, FIGURATIVE
TRADITION AND POP ART

FIRST BASEMENT

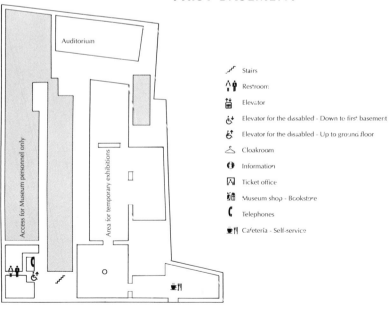

Auditorium

Access for Museum personnel only

Area for temporary exhibitions

⟋ Stairs

Restroom:

Elevator

Elevator for the disabled - Down to first basement

Elevator for the disabled - Up to ground floor

Cloakroom

Information

Ticket office

Museum shop - Bookstore

Telephones

Cafeteria - Self-service

Introduction

The works of art presented here have been brought together by two generations of the Thyssen-Bornemisza family. The collection, started in the twenties by Baron Heinrich, was considerably enlarged by his son Hans Heinrich, the present Baron Thyssen-Bornemisza.

In 1988 the Spanish government came to a loan agreement with the Thyssen-Bornemisza family which made it possible for the collection to be shown to the public in both Barcelona, in the Monastery of Pedralbes, and Madrid, in the Villahermosa Palace. Once the Palace had been remodelled, the Thyssen-Bornemisza Museum opened its doors to the public on 10 October 1992. A few months later, on 21 June 1993, an agreement was signed whereby the Spanish State acquired the collection, comprising 775 paintings.

Although a selection of 60 paintings are on view at the Monastery of Pedralbes in Barcelona, the remaining 715 works of the collection are exhibited in Madrid at the Villahermosa Palace. Additionally, both in Madrid and Barcelona, the exhibition is complemented by sculptures, *objets d'art* and paintings on loan from the private collection of Baron and Baroness Thyssen-Bornemisza.

The Villahermosa Palace, built at the turn of the 18th and 19th centuries, is an excellent example of the neoclassical architecture of Madrid. The building has been renovated and remodelled by the architect Rafael Moneo to adapt it for its use as a museum. In addition to the air-conditioning, lighting and security installations required for this new function, Rafael Moneo's project has redistributed the rooms and scheme of circulation of the Villahermosa Palace. The rooms, arranged around a large central covered courtyard, are of various sizes, with the largest ones perpendicular to the Paseo del Prado facade. The result is an interior architecture which, while fully modern, evokes the atmosphere of the palace and classical air of pre-20th century museums and art galleries.

The basement houses the cafeteria, the temporary exhibition rooms and the conference room. On the ground floor we find the great central courtyard, the lobby, the bookshop and the cloakroom.

The rest of this floor, and practically all of the second and third floors, house the permanent collection.

The collection is displayed according to chronological and historical criteria. The fact that the second-floor rooms have lower ceilings and enjoy natural, overhead lighting made it convenient to place there the oldest paintings, generally smaller in size. The visitor wishing to see the collection in its historical order must cross the courtyard and go up to the second floor in the lift or by the main staircase. The rooms are numbered to indicate the suggested tour, which follows an anticlockwise route around the courtyard, descending floor by floor.

Care has been taken to give the rooms the greatest possible stylistic unity; each one responds, so to speak, to a chapter in the history of art.

NB. In this guide technical information on the works has been reduced to a minimum. When an artist represented in the collection is mentioned for the first time, his (or her) dates of birth and death are given in brackets after the name. In some cases the titles of the works mentioned in the text are given in abbreviated form. At the end of the guide a list of all the works exhibited is given with comprehensive information, such as date of execution, technique, dimensions and catalogue number. When mentioned, the catalogue number is given as Cat. no. x. The letter A which sometimes appears in these references, for example Cat. A.x, denotes works belonging to the private collection of Baron and Baroness Thyssen-Bornemisza.

SECOND FLOOR

1 Early Italians

Vasari, the artist and art historian active in 16th-century Florence, presented the history of the artists now known as the 'Early Italians' (13th-15th century) as a rebirth of painting.

In Vasari's opinion, the visual arts had risen to their first great peak in the Classical world of Greece and Rome, only to decline with the fall of the Roman Empire. This decline was due to the move away from nature which typified the long reign of Byzantine art. For Vasari, the return to naturalism, which began to emerge with Giotto, signalled a rebirth of the visual arts.

The visitor can appreciate the contrast between what Vasari saw as the old style and the new style by comparing the *Madonna and Child* by the Master of the Magdalen (Cat. 256) with *Christ and the Samaritan Woman* by Duccio (Cat. 133). These works were both produced in Tuscany around 1300 and are separated by less than twenty years, but nonetheless represent two radically different approaches to painting. In the former, the holy figures are depicted frontally as if they were in a niche. In the latter, the painter attempts to depict a story (which the spectator will have heard, or read in the New Testament), and therefore places the characters in a setting which contains a certain amount of spatial depth. The former manner, the old style, required the painter (like any other craftsman) to master a limited repertoire of figures, strokes, forms, and colours. The conventions defining this repertoire left little room for innovation. In contrast, the latter manner required the artist to make a continual effort to extend the repertoire, using elements extracted from his observation of nature (human figures, buildings, everyday objects, items of clothing, gestures, facial expressions, etc.). In the old style, the criterion of perfection was predetermined, while in the new it remained open to a continual process of invention. The artist in the modern sense of the word had been born.

The need for the painting to be coherent despite its containing a multitude of disparate elements which were no longer predetermined gave rise to the concept of *composition*: the art of subordinating every part or element of the painting to the objective or the main effect pursued by the artist.

Imitation of nature, narrative, spatial depth, and composition formed the new basis for painting. We can distinguish historical periods, schools and individual artists from the extent to which each of these are developed, the degree of emphasis placed on one or another, and the idiosyncrasies of their interpreters.

133. Duccio di Buoninsegna
Christ and the Samaritan Woman, 1310-1311.

Tempera on panel on gold background. 43.5 x 46 cm.

Thus, within Tuscany, where the main current in Early Italian painting evolved, we can distinguish between the Florentine and Sienese Schools. The former, dominated by Giotto and his pupils, saw composition as the opposing and balancing of bodies, masses, volumes and gestures see for example the *Crucifixion* (Cat. 151) by Agnolo Gaddi, (active c. 1369-1396). For the Sienese school, where Duccio was accompanied at the outset by Simone Martini (c. 1284-1344), Pietro Lorenzetti (active between 1306? and 1345) and Ugolino di Nerio, composition was more than anything a question of harmonising colour -full of contrasts between densely saturated tones- and drawing, with its fluid, stylised line. While the Florentine current triumphed in the long run (more than anything due to the

development of perspective in the 15th century) the Sienese school exercised a greater immediate influence. This influence spread to other parts of Italy in the 14th century (see the *Crucifixion* (Cat. 425) by Vitale da Bologna, c. 1300-1359/60), and combined with the inclination towards narrative fantasy and emphasis on feeling to make a definitive contribution to forming the style known as International Gothic in the last quarter of the century. This style would continue to be practised in some places until the second half of the 15th century (see *St Catherine before the Pope at Avignon*, Cat. 162, by the Sienese painter Giovanni di Paolo, active c. 1369-1396).

162. **Giovanni di Paolo.**
St Catherine before the Pope at Avignon, early 1460s.

Tempera on panel. 29 x 29 cm.

425. Vitale da Bologna
The Crucifixion, c. 1335.

Tempera on panel. 93 x 51.2 cm.

2 Medieval Art

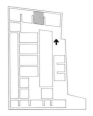

International Gothic, a homogeneous style of painting which combined Italian (especially Sienese) formulae with various regional styles, began to spread across the whole of Europe at the end of the 14th century. Its dominance was challeged by the emergence of the early Renaissance in the late 1420s, but the Renaissance revolution, which began in certain Italian and Netherlandish cities, spread slowly. It was not until the 16th century, or even the end of it in some countries, that it spread to all corners of Europe.

The reliefs carved in ivory displayed in this room are a good example of Gothic taste. These small works, which required highly refined craftsmanship, were greatly esteemed. The narrative formulae used to compose the scenes represented in them, which are almost always passages from Holy Scripture, perfectly illustrate the conventions of the age.

As for the paintings, the oldest in this room date from the mid-14th century, a time at which the pictorial language of Gothic was still neither uniform nor universal. This explains the singular style of the *Holy Visage of Christ Triptych* (Cat. 44) by Master Bertram (c. 1330/40-1414), an artist working in the Hamburg area.

During the course of the 15th century the cities became richer and the market for religious works expanded continuously. As a consequence of this expansion, the pictorial language of Gothic diversified into different regional and local schools. The eight panels dedicated to the four evangelists painted in the last third of the 15th century belong to the end of this stylistic cycle (Cat. 233 to 240). Their author, Gabriel Maelesskircher (c.1430/40-1495), practised in Munich, and Michael Wolgemut, later the master of Dürer, trained in his workshop.

The most representative work of late Gothic, and the most outstanding in the room, is the *Assumption of the Virgin* (Cat. 210) by Johann Koerbecke (c. 1420-1490). Painted shortly before 1457, this panel comes from an altarpiece produced for the Cistercian monastery of Marienfeld. Its author worked in the area of Münster, the city that was to be the scene of one of the most turbulent and bloodstained episodes of the Reformation scarcely two generations later. The intense and elegant expressiveness of the faces and gestures, the sumptuous colourings of the robes, the flamboyant composition, and the sinuous, flame-like quality of the lines all glow with the splendour of what Huizinga called the 'waning of the Middle Ages'.

210. **Johann Koerbecke**
The Assumption of the Virgin, shortly before 1457.

Oil on panel. 93.1 x 64.2 cm.

3 Early Netherlandish Artists

Set against a similar social background and conditioned by a similar cultural climate, the Netherlandish Renaissance in painting shared a basic imperative with that of Italy: the imitation of nature. The differences lie in the way this imperative was applied: the abstract, methodical painting of the early Renaissance in Italy concentrated on the conquest of space and culminated with the development of geometric perspective; Netherlandish painting was tactile and temperamental, and would incline towards a fascination for particularity of detail.

The systematic character of the Italian Renaissance allowed it to develop as a relatively impersonal programme with a clear sense of progress. In the Netherlands, the sense of progress is far less clear and the programme is defined by the personal styles of the great masters: the further we leave them or their workshops behind, the closer we come to the general Gothic background of the age.

The first of these masters is Jan van Eyck (c. 1390-1441), the legendary father of Netherlandish painting. The subject of the diptych in the Thyssen-Bornemisza Collection is the *Annunciation* (Cat. 137). The artist has decided to depict the Angel, the Virgin and the Holy Spirit not directly, but as sculptures. With elegant bearings and proportions, finely modelled, imbued with a beauty to which no living being could aspire, the figures are related to each other without truly forming a group. They have the appearance of high reliefs carved in a stone which has the hue of certain old silvers under the light. Their reflections appear on a background of black stone. The visual portrayl is so masterful that we can determine exactly which sort of stone is depicted.

Other 15th-century Netherlandish paintings on religious themes can be seen alongside this masterpiece. They form an exceptional group in terms of both quality and representiveness. Two of the most important ones are painted by Jacques Daret (active between 1418 and 1468) and Rogier van der Weyden (c. 1399-1464), the two main pupils of Robert Campin. The beautiful *Adoration* scene (Cat. 124) is by the former, a capital piece of work belonging to the group painted for the Abbey of St Vaast in Arras, and the only documented work by this artist. His contemporary, Van der Weyden, is represented by a *Madonna Enthroned* (Cat. 435) as small in size as it is monumental in appearance. Also very small is *Our Lady of the Dry Tree* (Cat. 121) by Petrus Christus (c. 1410-1472/73), this painting is one of the masterpieces of the

Collection. It represents a theological metaphor based on the Old Testament: the Virgin, who carries the Messiah, is like a flowering shoot with which God makes the dry tree of the chosen people green again. Twelve golden letter A's hang from the branches, symbolising, among other things, Hail Marys. This small panel may have been used as a private rosary.

Four other works of the highest quality belong to the last third of the century. The severe, heartfelt *Lamentation* (Cat. 142) by Juan de Flandes (active between 1496 and 1519) was painted in Spain. In the triptych on the same subject (Cat.252) by the Master of the St Lucy Legend (active c. 1475-c. 1501), the tragic eloquence the artist learned from his master, Van der Weyden, is softened by the Italian

137.a-b. **Jan van Eyck**
The Annunciation Diptych, c.1435-1441.

Oil on panel. Each panel: 39 x 24 cm.

influence felt in Bruges at that time. In contrast with this work, the *Crucifixion* (Cat. 270) by the Master of the Virgo Inter Virgines (active between 1480 and 1495), painted around 1487, with its crowded composition, its exuberant colouring and its narrative density, offers a magnificent testimony of the survival of Gothic taste in the peripheral regions of the Netherlands. Also archaistic, although in a very different sense, is the no less magnificent Crucifixion by Gerard David. The most Italian-influenced and last of the master painters of the golden age of Bruges deliberately looks back to the past in order to evoke the splendid manner of Van Eyck, Campin and Van der Weyden.

124. **Jacques Daret**
The Nativity, 1434-35.

Oil on panel. 60 x 53 cm.

121. Petrus Christus
Our Lady of the Dry Tree, c. 1450.

Oil on panel.17.4 x 12.3 cm.

4 The Italian Quattrocento

The Majority of the works gathered in this room are from the north of Italy. The most outstanding exception is a Neapolitan *Crucifixion* that must for the moment be considered anonymous (Cat. 94). The tragic intensity of the expressions, the density of the colour and the fluidity of the brushwork reveal a strong Flemish influence. In contrast, the spatial arrangement of the figures and the sharpness of the city and the mountains stretching into the distance are undoubtedly Italian. Attributed for a time to Colantonio, the master of Antonello da Messina, specialists now look to an as yet undetermined French or Flemish master working in Naples during the reign of Alfonso V.

A significant group of the paintings exhibited here are ascribed to the school of Ferrara, a city whose ducal court was an important literary and artistic centre during the second half of the 15th century and the first decades of the 16th century. There is a beautiful scene from the voyage of the Argonauts taken from Ovid (Cat. 344) by Ercole de'Roberti (c. 1450-1496). The representation of a mythological subject in painting at such an early date could only have been produced within the minority circles of courtly humanism.

This outstanding product of the Ferrarese school and the presence of certain artists from Veneto (Zoppo, 1433-1478, and Alvise Vivarini, c. 1445-c. 1505) tie in with the magnificent offering of Venetian painting at the beginning of the 16th century in room 7. However, the most important work in this room points us in another direction. Probably painted in the last decade of the century, it offers that synthesis of perspective, drawing (Mantegna), volume and colour (Antonello) that Dürer was to admire in Giovanni Bellini during the same period. But there is nothing of the Venetian in this *Man of Sorrows* (Cat. 61), as masterfully idealised as it is unforgettably tangible and present. Attributed for a time to Bramante, the critics are now inclining towards his pupil, Bartolomeo Suardi, known as Bramantino (c. 1465-1530). Comparison with the Neapolitan Crucifixion mentioned above reveals just how much progress had been made since the convergence of Italian and Flemish painting four decades before: we are now on the threshold of the High Renaissance.

61. **Bramantino**
The Ressurrected Christ.

Oil on panel. 109 x 73 cm.

It is no coincidence that the portrait was invented during the Renaissance. The primary function of medieval painting was to present characters from holy scripture and their deeds: it was a question of attempting to depict something which could not be seen in everyday life. To make the object of painting the depiction not of the supernatural or marvellous but of everyday reality represented an important cultural transformation.

Otherwise, the fact that the portrait was the first (chronologically and in order of importance) of the worldly themes taken up by Renaissance painting can be seen as a symptom of the profound change in values that the Renaissance brought with it. This was precisely the change noted by Jacob Burckhardt when he made the development of the individual one of the basic themes of his famous essay published in 1860, *The Civilisation of the Renaissance in Italy*.

This did not prevent the portrait from being used for different practical purposes. For a long time it was associated with religious painting: the donors of an altarpiece, for instance, might have themselves painted as onlookers piously witnessing the events of the religious scene and it is difficult to imagine that their religious sentiments were not accompanied by a desire to leave a visual record of their identity and appearance for contemporaries and perhaps for posterity. Once painting had become such a faithful visual record of personality and physical appearance it could also be used for other purposes. The painting of prospective marriage partners provides a good example. Marriages were sometimes arranged for political or economic reasons without the future bride and groom's knowing each other or ever having met. In such circumstances the fathers or go-betweens sometimes employed a painter to dispel the unders-tandable anxieties of the future couple. At the end of the 15th century the cultural habit of painting prospective marriage partners was extended and transformed, giving rise in some European countries to the double portrait of the married couple. In other cases (for example in Venice) the client might simply commission a portrait of his beloved.

Personality and physical appearance, the visible and the spiritual aspects of beauty; the Latin epigram of the poet Martial inscribed in the portrait of Giovanna Tornabuoni by the Florentine painter Domenico Ghirlandaio (Cat 158) played on this duality: 'If the artist had been able to portray the character and moral qualities,

18. Antonello da Messina
Portrait of a Man, c. 1475 - 1476.

Mixed media on panel. 27.5 x 21 cm.

74. Robert Campin
Portrait of a Stout Man
(Robert de Masmines?), c. 1425(?).

Oil on panel. 35.4 x 23.7 cm.

284.a. Hans Memling
Young Man at Prayer, c. 1485

Oil on panel. 29 x 22.5 cm.

141. Juan de Flandes
Portrait of an Infanta
(Catherine of Aragon?), c. 1496.

Oil on canvas. 31.5 x 22 cm.

The Early
Renaissance Portrait

there would not be a more beautiful painting in the world'. Leaving aside the elements of social convention and play, there is something deep down in this elegant Latin quotation that is of interest to us here: the conviction of Renaissance man that there must be a deep correspondence between physical perfection and spiritual perfection. In the end, it is this conviction which explains the enormous importance attained by art in the Renaissance; if painting could capture physical beauty as if in a mirror, it should be possible to capture spiritual beauty in the same way.

The mirror of beauty represented by the portrait of Giovanna Tornabuoni is accompanied in this room by twelve other masterful portraits from the early Renaissance: five Flemish, five Italian, one German and one Spanish-Flemish.

The oldest Flemish and Italian paintings should perhaps not strictly be considered portraits. The *Monk Holding Cross* (Cat. 130) painted by Domenico Veneziano (1400/10-1461) in the 1440s represents, according to a probable hypothesis, St Philip Benizi, head of the Servite order, who died at the end of the 13th century. The painter could not conceivably have had access to a visual likeness of the saint, and probably resorted to a contemporary model. In contrast, it is reasonable to suppose that the posthumous *Portrait of Wenceslas, Duke of Brabant* (Cat. 11), painted around 1405, is indeed a portrait, even though the sitter had died in 1383. We can be sure that his likeness had been preserved in drawings. Comparison between this work and that of Domenico Veneziano, done almost four decades later, reveals how much more developed the art of portraiture was in the Netherlands than in Italy in the first half of the 15th century.

The most striking confirmation of this superiority can be seen in the portrait of *Robert de Masmines* (Cat. 74) painted by Robert Campin before 1430. In this work, predating Van Eyck's *Annunciation Diptych* (see Room 3) by a few years, the great master has constructed the head of the Burgundian soldier with the same obsession for exactitude as a craftsman making a high precision instrument.

In order to find an Italian portrait that does not pale in comparison with Campin's we have to await Antonello da Messina's most brilliant period, his Venetian sojourn during the 1470s (Cat 18). As little as this head of a young Italian concedes in exactness to the prodigious work of the Flemish master the more it probably gains in

ARS VTINAM MORES
ANIMVM QVE EFFINGERE
POSSES PVLCHRIOR IN TER
RIS NVLLA TABELLA FORET
MCCCCLXXXVIII

158. Domenico Ghirlandaio
Portrait of Giovanna Tornabuoni, 1488.
Mixed media on panel. 77 x 49 cm.

The Early
Renaissance Portrait

architecture, clarity of volume and, of course, in the treatment of the light. But these were new times, the technique of oil painting had been enriched and the tastes of the collectors and lovers of painting had changed. In this last third of the 15th century, Flanders, or more precisely, Bruges, offers us another portrait with masterful lighting, in this case by Memling (c. 1435-1494) (an artist from the same generation as Antonello). The precision in colour is even greater, and it is bathed in a more delicate light than that of Antonello, although the latter wins out in terms of volumetric precision and rotundity (Cat. 284).

The selection of portraits assembled in this room concludes with two masterpieces already belonging to the 16th century, the portraits of two contemporary figures drawn from the royal families of Castile and England. They are stylistically conservative. The Flemish style of the first half of the previous century is revived in both, filtered in the case of the *Portrait of an Infanta (Catherine of Aragon?)* by Juan de Flandes (Cat. 141) by a gentle melancholia and highly personal use of colour, and in the case of Hans Holbein's (1497/8-1543) *Portrait of King Henry VIII* (Cat. 191) by the splendour of a monarch emanating learning, power, wealth and youth. Painted in an age in which new horizons were opening up in painting in Florence, Rome and Venice, these two works splendidly conclude one of the most fascinating chapters in the history of painting.

19¹. Hans Holbein, The Younger
Portrait of King Henry VIII, c. 1534-36.

Oil on panel. 28 x 20 cm.

6 Villahermosa Gallery

Alongside the major arts, traditionally considered to be painting and sculpture, we find the minor or decorative arts. They represent a significant part of the history of art, perhaps the most sensitive to the influence of fashions and changes in taste.

The chronology of the German gold and silverwork displayed in this gallery allows us to follow the diffusion of Renaissance taste. A noteworthy item is the *Imhoff Standing Cup* (Cat. 082), which bears the emblem of this Nuremberg family—a lion with a fish's tail. The master Hans Petzolt (1551-1633) has demonstrated great skill in the illustrations carved on the main body of the cup, consisting of six mining scenes. These are complemented by allegorical representations of the four elements and the four seasons on the stem and the lid respectively. The extraordinary *Covered Standing Cup* (Cat. 081) crowned by a warrior also merits attention for the richness of the work and the colouring of the precious stones. Its creator, Veit Moringer, who became a master in 1535, employs a vertical decoration, drawing inspiration for some of the reliefs from the engravings which were widely circulated at the time.

The famous antique group of the *Laocoön* made a very strong impression on artists after its discovery in Rome in 1506. The theme is employed by Pierre Reymond (active between 1534 and 1578) in his decoration of a large Limoges enamelware dish (Cat. E13) which is finished, on its circular borders, with grotesques entwined with masks, all of this within the most characteristic Mannerist style.

In the field of sculpture, the *Annunciation* (Cat. S50. 1–2) group by the sculptor and architect Sansovino (1486-1570) is worthy of note. Born in Florence and active in Rome until 1527, after the sacking of the city Sansovino moved to Venice, where he established a close friendship with Titian and became the city's leading architect. The beauty of its proportions and the elegance of its line make this work, which was probably executed during the 1540s, a magnificent example of the mature Venetian Renaissance.

0 81. Veit Moringer
Covered standing Cup, c.1555-69

Silver, gilt. Height: 35 cm.

E 13. Pierre Reymond
Large Dish, 16th century.

Enamel and copper. Ø 40.5 cm.

0 82. Hans Petzolt
The Imhoff Standing Cup, 1626 .

Silver, gilt.Height: 46.3 cm.

S 50. 1-2. Jacopo Sansovino
The Annunciation, c. 1535.

Terracotta, painted in polychrome. Height: 85 cm.

33

7 16th-Century Italian Painting

No school or artistic period has exerted an influence comparable with that of the High Renaissance. Its main centre was Rome, although the activity of Florentine artists, humanists and patrons in the city was decisive to the overall synthesis. The artistic formulae of the High Renaissance spread from Italy to the rest of Europe and ended up becoming the Classical canon for the teaching of painting, sculpture and architecture.

However, the richness of 16th-century Italy is not limited to the Classicism of Rome; the Venetian school continued to prosper for the first three decades of the century, and its influence on subsequent painting, whilst more intermittent, was at least as rich as that of Rome.

In order to complete the picture we must add the complex web of Mannerism, which succeeded the High Renaissance in Rome, Florence, and other regions of the peninsula, and the new Bolognese Classicism, which arose in the last quarter of the century.

The works assembled in this room offer a broad view of the richness of Italian painting during the 16th century.

The first work to draw our attention is the *Young Knight in a Landscape* Cat. 82) by the Venetian Vittore Carpaccio, one of the gems of the Collection. It is generally considered a portrait, but if it is we do not know the identity of the young knight. Nor do we know the precise significance of the animals, plants, and other allegorical figures inhabiting the background landscape. It may be related to some public or military event of the period. In any case, it can be safely supposed that the aim of the painter and the wish of the client was to represent the subject as the incarnation of a young Christian warrior with all the virtues and qualities attributed to the heroes of the tales of chivalry popular at the time. It is certainly one of the greatest works of Carpaccio (c. 1460/65-1525/26), a painter with an extraordinary ability for invoking images from the collective imagination of his time. Painted in 1510, it has a greater stylistic affinity with the painting of the previous century than with that of the new; it is easy to see this by comparing it with Gentile Bellini's *Annunciation* (Cat. 38) dated around 1470, which has been exhibited in this room precisely for its relationship with the work of his student, Carpaccio.

The school of Gentile Bellini (1430-1516), important as it was in the early years of the century, came to an end after the death of Carpaccio. That of his brother Giovanni, on the other hand was the

82. **Vittore Carpaccio**
Young Knight in a Landscape, 1510.

Oil on canvas. 218.5 x 151.5 cm.

source of the main current, which lasted practically until the end of the century. The *Nunc Dimittis* (Cat. 39) is by Giovanni Bellini, a work which the specialists have dated differently, although practically always within the first decade of the century. The frontal view, internal coherence and static nature of the composition and the fullness of the forms evoke the formal values of Roman low-reliefs; this painting thus reveals the new Classicism that Giovanni Bellini introduced to Venice in 1505 with the great San Zaccaria Altarpiece and which was to be the point of departure for his disciples Giorgione (c. 1476/8-1510), Sebastiano dei Piombo and Titian. In any case, the degree of psychological abstraction in the characters, the gentleness of the landscape and the fading of volume to achieve a warmer and more transparent colouring evoke the painter's late period.

Although painted in Rome around 1511 or 1512, the magnificent *Portrait of Ferry Carondolet* (Cat. 369), one of Sebastiano del Piombo's best works, is still full of Venetian influence—the monumentality of the composition and the volumetry reveal the Classicism introduced by Bellini and practised in Giorgione's workshop, where Sebastiano worked between 1505 and 1510.

Palma Il Vecchio (c. 1480-1528) was also a pupil of Giovanni Bellini, from whom he derived the prototype for the *Sacra Conversazione* exhibited here. This work, produced around 1522, six years after the death of the Master, is composed with greater variety and movement, in consonance with the new taste introduced by Titian with his great compositions in the Church of Saint Mary the Glorious. Also close to Titian (it was attributed to him for some time) is the portrait of *La Bella* (Cat. 310, exhibited in Room 6). It is dated circa 1525. We do not know the identity of the subject, but we know that portraits were sometimes painted and bought simply for their beauty or visual splendour at that time in Venice.

The panorama of Venetian painting in this room concludes with another portrait by Titian (c. 1490-1576) dated circa 1555, the official portrait of the Doge Francesco Vernier (Cat. 405). Although the scheme of composition has varied very little from what we saw in Sebastiano practically half a century before, the manner of painting is totally different: we no longer see the great swathes of colour which characterised Venetian painting in the first two decades of the century and, although the palette is limited, the basic

369. Sebastiano del Piombo
Portrait of Ferry Carondolet with his Secretaries, 1510-1512.

Oil on panel. 112.5 x 87 cm.

330. Raphael
*Portrait of a young Man
(¿Alessandro de Medicis?), c. 1515*

Oil on panel. 43.8 x 29 cm.

145. Pierfrancesco di Jacopo Foschi
Portrait of a Lady, 1530-1535.

Oil on panel. 101 x 79 cm.

310. Palma il Vecchio
*Portrait of a Young Woman
"La Bella", c. 1525*

Oil on canvas. 95 x 80 cm.

colours (dark earths, purple and gold) fragment into an infinity of diverse tones. The results of this pictorial revolution can be seen in Room 11.

The Venetian school is the best represented in this room, but two interesting compositions by Piero di Cosimo (1461/62-1527) and Fra Bartolomeo (1472-1517) (Cat. 320 and 29 respectively) transport us to the Florence of the early 16th century. However, the most outstanding painting is from Rome: the *Portrait of a Young Man* produced by Raphael (1483-1520) towards the end of the second decade (Cat. 330). While the perfection of the drawing and the subtlety of the colouring are characteristic of the Raphaelesque synthesis, the marvellous spontaneity and grace of execution recall the Venetian qualities which seem to have influenced the master in his last years.

After its culmination in the High Renaissance, Italian painting underwent a profound change of course, which has been dubbed Mannerism by recent historiography. Three important works assembled here allow us to appreciate the characteristics of the new style. The *Madonna and Child with St John and St Jerome* (Cat. 33) by the Sienese painter Domenico Beccafumi (1486-1551) is perhaps the most spectacular. The tight, contrasting composition, the extremely sinuous lines and, more than anything, the vivid colours are symptomatic of the fever of innovation that began to grip Italian painting in the 1520s. The deformations of perspective and the warm but contained atmosphere of the *Portrait of a Young Man as St Sebastian* (Cat. 64) by Bronzino (1503-1572) or the cold elegance and skillful geometrical games of the *Portrait of a Lady* by Pierfrancesco Foschi (1502-1567) (Cat. 145) reveal other facets of the Mannerist transformation.

33. Domenico Beccafumi
Madonna and Child with St. John and St. Jerome, c. 1523-1524.

Oil on panel.Ø 85.5 cm.

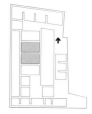

The Gothic currents covered in Room 3 did not disappear from the German sphere until the end of the 15th century. Good examples of this can be seen in the works of the anonymous master active in Düren (Cat. 259) and the Master of Grossgmain (Cat. 250). This survival of Gothic was accompanied by a slow penetration of Flemish and Italian influences. Thus, in the *Madonna with St Margaret and St Catherine* (Cat. 308) by a follower of Michael Pacher (1430/35-1498) the mastery of perspective and almost Ferarese elegance of the figures are seen against a traditional gold ground.

The characteristic traditionalism of German religious painting at the beginning of the 16th century may be explained by the fact that its clientele was formed by the urban petit bourgeoisie. Nonetheless, this stylistic conservatism could produce works of great skill and enormous visual impact, such as the magnificent *Calvary* by Derick Baegert (c. 1440-c. 1515). This work was dismembered and the fragments dispersed. The five surviving fragments exhibited here (Cat. 22–26) were patiently acquired for the Thyssen-Bornemisza Collection during the thirties.

Other outstanding religious works exhibited here include the expressive *Annunciation to St Anne* by Bernhard Strigel (1460-1528) (Cat. 380) and the *Heavenly Rosary Triptych* by Hans Kulmbach (1485-1521) (Cat. 212.a–c), in which the artist imposes a composition striving towards the Classical on a subject treated allegorically in the medieval manner. In the *The Nativity* by Barthel Bruyn the Elder (1493-1555) (Cat. 69) Italian influences blend with the Netherlandish, an effect even more clearly visible in the portraits of a man and wife (Cat. 67 and 68). A similar fusion of Italian and Netherlandish elements can be seen in the *The Virgin with Child Eating Grapes* by Lucas Cranach the Elder (1472-1553) (Cat. 114). Painted in the first decade of the 16th century, the intensity of the colour and the expressiveness of the landscape link this painting with the style of the so-called Danube School.

Dürer (1471-1528) is the most outstanding of all these artists, the key figure of the German Renaissance. According to an inscription next to the signature, his panel *Jesus among the Doctors* (Cat. 134) dated 1506 was painted in the brief period of five days. The variety of figures and the novelty of the composition give it the air of a challenge, as if Dürer was stimulated by the artistic environment of Italy to produce the best of which he was capable. The half-length figures crowded around the young Jesus appear to

114. Lucas Cranach, the Elder

The Virgin with Child eating Grapes, c. 1509-1510.

Oil on panel. 71.5 x 44.2 cm.

16th-Century
German Painting

be inspired by Leonardo da Vinci. The youthful hands of Jesus and the old ones of his main opponent form an energetically drawn group that the painter has placed in the centre of the composition.

The coming of the Reformation in the first quarter of the 16th century and the conflicts which followed it in Germany had a deep influence on the history of German painting. One of the first consequences of this crucial historic event was that the church ceased to commission paintings.

The paintings in these rooms by Lucas Cranach the Elder (one of whose religious works from his early period was mentioned above) and his sons Hans (c. 1513-1537) and Lucas the Younger (1515-1586) illustrate the dominant taste in painting during the first years of the Reformation in one of the main princely courts of the Empire, that of the Elector of Saxony. The most outstanding is the *Reclining Nymph* (Cat. 115), who is stretched out in front of a pool fed by a stream of water. This subject has been connected with the spring of Castalia, a source of inspiration for poets and philosophers, and with the sleeping Venus. The bow and arrows of Cupid are hanging from the branch of a tree. While the subject matter, with its strong Neo-Platonic influence, evokes Italian humanism, it is difficult to imagine a bigger contrast than the one between the styles of painting of the two countries.

Perhaps the most intense examples of this 16th-century German style are those of Hans Baldung Grien (1484/85-1545), an artist who trained with Dürer and who was close in style to Cranach. He painted an *Adam and Eve* (Cat. 27), where the theme of original sin is treated with a degree of sensuality, and the *Portrait of a Woman* (Cat. 28). In this outstanding portrait, a woman who corresponds to the typology created by Cranach, lit by a powerful source of light which paradoxically brings out the softness of the modelling, gazes at us with an enigmatic look. The effect that the painter achieves with a restricted palette apparently consisting of no more than a green, two reds, white and black is astonishing.

With the disappearance of religious painting, the portrait finally became the dominant genre in 16th-century German painting. The ample selection contained in the Thyssen-Bornemisza Collection allows us to follow its evolution from its origins in the last part of the previous century.

This ample selection contains a prototype of the portrait with an imaginary background, the *Portrait of Levinus Memminger* (Cat.

134. **Albrecht Dürer**
Jesus Among the Doctors, 1506.

Oil on panel. 64.3 x 80.3 cm.

440), a personage connected with the city of Nuremberg, by Michael Wogemut (1434/37-1519). The *Portrait of a Man* by Bernhard Strigel takes the same form. Hans Wertinger (c. 1465/70-1533) with the *Portrait of a Dwarf 'Knight Christoph'* (Cat. 434) dated 1515, contributes one of the first full-length portraits to the history of painting.

The Collection also includes other typologies, such as the double portraits of *Coloman Helmschild and his Wife Agnes Breu* (Cat. 244) by Breu the Elder (c. 1480-1537) and an anonymous painter. The couple are set in semi-circular arches. Barthel Beham, a famous Munich painter, in his two panels with the *Portrait of Ruprecht Stüpf* and *Ursula Rudolph* (Cat. 36 and 37) portrays this patrician couple in more than half-length, playing in the composition with the curtains adorning the background.

In the mysterious *Portrait of a Woman* (Cat. 2) with its contrasting colour scheme, Albrecht Altdorfer (c. 1480-1538), the

creator of the Danube School, employs the three-quarter-length at a relatively early date. Christoph Amberger (c. 1502-1562), a painter who knew Titian, leads us more directly to the tastes and requirements of the clients with his *Portrait of Matthäus Schwarz* (Cat. 4), where numerous details speak to us of the personality of the Fuggers' accountant.

FONTIS NYMPHA SACRI SOMNVM
NE RVMPE QVIESCO.

115. Lucas Cranach, the Elder
Reclining Nymph, c. 1530-34.

Oil on panel. 75 x 120 cm.

28. Hans Baldung Grien
Portrait of a Woman, 1530(?).

Oil on panel. 69.2 x 52.5 cm.

10 16th-Century Netherlandish Painting

The 16th century is generally considered a period of transition between the two most glorious eras of Netherlandish painting. During its course, values mentioned above, such as the taste for a highly realistic and detailed representation of everyday reality, a love of nature and its elements, rigour in drawing, Northern light or the saturated colouring used by the early painters in the 15th century, were gradually joined by the new Renaissance concepts in painting arriving from Italy.

Thus, painters such as Gossaert, Van Orley (c. 1488-1541), Lucas van Leyden (c. 1494-1533) and Van Cleve (c. 1485-1541) introduced a new language. Jan Gossaert (1478-1533/36), represented in the collection with an *Adam and Eve* (Cat. 163) full of symbolic flowers and plants, was one of the first painters to cultivate the nude. We do not know the full significance of Lucas van Leyden's painting of a woman playing cards with two gentlemen. Joachim Patinir (c. 1485-1524) deserves mention alongside these artists for his importance as the precursor of landscape painting. In the *Landscape with the Rest on the Flight to Egypt* (Cat. 314) we see an imaginary landscape dominated by blue-green tones.

A large group of painters known as the 'Antwerp Mannerists', whose style was based on a renewal of the old, deserve separate mention. Jan de Beer (c. 1475-c. 1536) with his two panels *The Birth of the Virgin* and *The Annunciation* (Cat. 34 and 35), where the elongated figures in unstable poses are dressed in flowing robes, may be one of the most famous exponents of this style.

The followers of Raphael, known as the 'Romanists', are represented in the Collection with a small work by Jan van Scorel (1495-1562). Another follower, whose work belongs to a more exalted or erudite Mannerism, was Maerten van Heemskerck (1498-1574) whose *Portrait of a Lady with Spindle and Distaff* draws us into an interior which reflects the everyday life of the personage. She is placed in the foreground with great monumentality, while the artist appears to take great pleasure in the representation of the diverse colours and objects he places around her.

183. **Maerten van Heemskerck**
Portrait of a Lady with Spindle and Distaff, c. 1531.

Oil on panel. 105 x 86 cm.

11 Titian, Tintoretto, Bassano and El Greco

The changes in Titian's painting in the middle years of the century gave rise to one of the greatest stylistic revolutions in the history of art. If we had to date its beginning we could cite the journey he made to Rome in 1545. The meeting with Michelangelo, whose great fresco of the *Last Judgement* had recently been unveiled, seems to have given Titian an even greater confidence in himself. It is significant that he painted the *Danaë*, now exhibited in the Museo di Capodimonte of Naples, during this visit. Justifying the liberty he took in painting the mythological figures, Titian declared that he created them in the manner of a poet rather than a story-teller. This explanation could be extended to his new way of applying colour. Vasari, who visited him in his studio in Venice in 1566, provides the following explanation: 'The manner he employs in his latest paintings is very different to that of his youth they are executed with bold, sweeping strokes, with the result that little can be seen in them when viewed from nearby, but viewed from a distance, they appear perfect. The method he uses is judicious, beautiful, and astonishing, because it makes the paintings appear alive and painted with great skill, but conceals the effort'.

Although few basic colours are used, each of them is divided into hundreds of tones dispersed all over the painting. The result is that it is impossible to isolate neutral areas. Just as all the melodies came together to develop the central theme in the great polyphonic works of the age, the different parts of the painting, following the same chromatic harmonies, came together to produce a poetic effect in accordance with the character of the subject represented.

Titian's *St Jerome in the Wilderness* (Cat. 406), although based on a previous version done twenty years before, was painted in the last years of the artist's life. The saint meditates on the Passion of Christ in the solitude of the wilderness. The bundle of sticks on the ground and the stone in his hand indicate that he is a penitent. In the undergrowth, the green strokes of certain leaves echo those mortifying the torso of the saint. The purple of his mantle extends in zigzag along the main diagonal of the composition; on the lower right-hand side, the powerful head of the lion melts into the shadow, while on the upper right-hand side, the light is lost in the undergrowth. A wind of desolation blows across the living and inanimate forms, blending them together.

Titian's change in style had an effect on the entire history of painting, from Rubens to Watteau and the last paintings of Cézanne.

406. Titian
Saint Jerome in the Wilderness, c. 1575.

Oil on canvas. 135 x 96 cm.

Titian, Tintoretto, Bassano and El Greco

It is therefore not surprising that it transformed Venetian painting in the second half of the century. The influence of the late Titian can be seen in the poetic force of the dark blues in the *Pastoral Landscape* (Cat. 31) by Jacopo Bassano (c. 1515-1592) and the glorious spiral of light and blessed spirits of Tintoretto's *Paradise* (Cat. 403, exhibited in the central gallery).

The painting of El Greco also exhibits the influence of Titian. *The Annunciation* (Cat. 172) painted in Venice derives its composition from an Annunciation painted by Titian in 1537. The influence of Mannerism is also patent here. The development of both influences and the maturing of the artist's powerful personality in Toledo produced one of the most intense and outstanding styles of painting in all the history of art. It was to culminate at the turn of the century, isolating his work from the new artistic currents emanating from Italy. Examples of this style exhibited here are the sketch of the *Annunciation* (Cat. 171) and *The Immaculate Conception* (Cat. 170).

403. **Tintoretto**
Paradise, c. 1583

Oil on canvas. 164 x 492 cm.

171. El Greco
Annunciation, 1596-1600.

Oil on canvas. 114 x 67 cm.

12 Early Baroque: Caravaggio and Bernini

In the last decades of the 16th century, Rome recovered the role of universal capital of the arts which it had lost after being sacked in 1527. This rebirth was associated with a new style, Baroque, which dominated the artistic life of Catholic Europe during the entire 17th century and a large part of the following one. The works assembled in this room illustrate the first stage of its development, which lasted until the third decade of the 17th century.

The emergence of the new style can be explained either in terms of the alternation of styles (Wölfflin), or in doctrinal terms, as a response to the religious principles of the Counter-Reformation (Weisbach). Both the conclusions of the Council of Trent and the recommendations propagated by the new religious orders of the Counter-Reformation (principally the Oratory and the Jesuits) required that works of art: 1) Be clear and intelligible; 2) should emotionally stimulate faith; 3) be true to life or 'realistic'. These requirements may be understood as the impulse which gave rise to a new style that contrasted with the artificiality, cold intellectualism and complexity of late Mannerism.

Although the painting of Caravaggio (1571-1610) met the requirements of the new taste, there were many obstacles to its being accepted in its time. This resistance has been traditionally attributed to the excessive realism of his figures, which were ultimately irreconcilable with the doctrinal principles of the Classical tradition. It must be stated, however, that Caravaggio's paintings evoke not so much the reality of the street but rather the fiction of the theatre or the *tableau vivant*.

Dated within the last five years of the 16th century, the *St Catherine of Alexandria* (Cat 81) exhibited here is a work from his youth. Wittkower has related it to the Flemish still-life tradition, the influence of which can be seen in some of the Master's previous works. There is indeed something of the still life in the contrasting textures of the brocades which occupy such a large part of the canvas, the white material of her blouse, the blade of the sword and her index finger resting on it. The knuckles are surprisingly pronounced (as Longhi observed) for a young woman with such a delicate neck.

Despite his enormous impact, Caravaggio's influence was not transmitted by an organised school. The works assembled in this room and room 20 reveal the diversity amongst the so-called Northern Caravaggisti. An even greater gap exists between them and the Spaniard José de Ribera (1591-1652), who took the stylistic

81. Caravaggio
Saint Catherine of Alexandria, c. 1597.

Oil on canvas.173 x 133 cm.

S 51. **Giovanni Lorenzo Bernini**
Saint Sebastian, 1615.

Marble. Height: 98.8 cm.

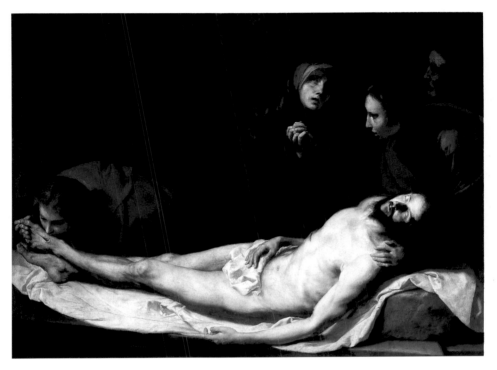

336. **Jusepe de Ribera**
Lamentation over the Body of Christ, 1633.

Oil on canvas. 157 x 210 cm.

principles of naturalism and harsh lighting commonly associated with Caravaggio further than anyone else. However, the *Lamentation* dated 1623 exhibited here already reveals the transition towards High Baroque which was occurring at the time in Naples.

In this transition, which had taken place ten years earlier in Rome (see *Lot and His Daughters* by Oracio Gentileschi, 1563-1639, Cat. 155), the influence of Giovanni Lorenzo Bernini (1598-1680) was decisive. The *St Sebastian* (Cat. S51) exhibited here was executed in 1615 when the artist was only seventeen years of age. His adaptation of serpentine composition to a seated figure owes a great deal to late Mannerism (and in the last instance, to Michelangelo). However, the elegance of the execution and the authority of its line already announce the great turning point which was to transform the clarity, verisimilitude and emotional immediacy of early Baroque into the exuberance, sensuality and grandiloquence of High Baroque.

These rooms cover the development of the new style, the birth of which we witnessed in room 12. The point of departure can be taken as the influence of Caravaggio and the development of naturalism. Following this thread, the works of Salini, Fetti, and two artists connected with Naples, Preti and Giordano, are presented here.

In his *Young Peasant with Flask* (Cat. 363) Tommaso Salini (c. 1575-1625) takes up a popular subject of simple composition where the harsh light reveals part of the face and torso of a boy. In the foreground the same light falls on some cabbages. This painting provides a reference for two genres which appear with naturalism and which would be widely developed in the 17th century: the still-life and the genre painting.

Domenico Fetti is (1589-1624) an eclectic painter in whose style the new naturalistic lighting plays with the colouring of the

176. **Guercino**
Christ and the Samaritan Woman at the Well, 1640-1641.

Oil on canvas. 116 x 156 cm.

327. **Mattia Preti**
A Concert, c. 1630-1640.

Oil on canvas. 107 x 145 cm.

great Venetian masters of the previous century. His two small panels *The Good Samaritan* and *The Parable of the Sower* (Cat. 139 and 140) illustrate two episodes from the New Testament; his subject matter is connected with the world of the Counter-Reformation.

Naples was to be an exceptionally important centre of naturalism, which was initially established there by Caravaggio and subsequently developed by the Spaniard Ribera. The latter was the teacher of Luca Giordano (1632-1705), who is represented by the large *Judgement of Solomon* (Cat. A 807). Although this is a work from his youth, the artist already displays his legendary talent. Along with the clearly Riberesque notes in the style (observe the pronounced realism of some of the faces) the scale of the figures is very noticeable. Two works by Mattia Preti (1613-1699), also trained in Naples, are exhibited. In *A Concert* (Cat. 327) three

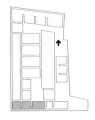

half-length characters are grouped around a table against a neutral background. The light, which falls strongly on parts of their faces, reveals a low range of colours. The artist's interest in such profane subject matter can be linked with his Roman period and in particular with the influence of the Northern artists, who were very numerous there in the first decades of the century.

Giovanni Francesco Barbieri, known as 'Il Guercino' (1591-1666), is one of the most outstanding artists of the second generation of Bolognese Classicism. *Jesus and the Samaritan Woman at the Well* (Cat. 176) presents figures drawn with great perfection and painted with soft contrasts in lighting. An excellent treatment of the textures can be appreciated in this painting, as in the pitcher the Samaritan woman is holding and the clothing of the personages.

17th-century French painting, centered in Paris and Rome, developed along the lines of a Baroque heavily influenced by Classicism. This did not stop certain artists from opting for realism. This is the case with the three members of the Le Nain family, Antoine (1600/10-1648), Louis (1593-1648) and Matthieu (1607-1677), whose generally small-scale compositions reflect the life of the French peasant, as in the *The Young Musicians* (Cat. 218) in room 13.

The French Classical current had its main base in Italy. Claude Gellée (1600-1682), known as Le Lorrain or Lorena, settled in Rome in 1627. He is the creator of a type of landscape with broad panoramas which nostalgically evoke the Classical world. *Pastoral Landscape with a Flight into Egypt* (Cat. 226) is typical of his interpretation of the Roman Campagna. The horizons of these landscapes are flooded with a ruddy crepuscular light. In the foregrounds and against the light the painter places masses of trees or Classical ruins which frame the scene like the borders in an Italian theatre.

With Valdés Leal (1622-1690) and Murillo (1617-1682) one of the richest centres of Spanish painting arose in the Seville of the second half of the century. *The Madonna and Saints with St Rosalina of Palermo* (Cat. 296), the work of Bartolomé Esteban Murillo sums up the most characteristic style of the master in the final stage of his career. The composition is simple: the central group arranged in a triangle is completed on the left by a secondary scene illustrating the life of the saint, possibly based on a view of Seville. Cherubim and martyrs painted with a free

296. Bartolomé Esteban Murillo
*Madonna and Child with Saint Rosalina of Palermo, c. *670.*

Oil on canvas. 190 x 147 cm.

stroke, their forms diluted by the treatment of light and colour, complete this delicate canvas probably painted for an altar. The work illustrates perfectly the brilliant eclectic style of this painter whose talent for communicating feeling was appreciated not only in his own time in the atmosphere of the late Counter-Reformation, but also much later, and from extremely diverse viewpoints, by the Romantics.

59. **Sebastien Bourdon**
The Holy Family, With Saint Elisabeth and Saint John the Baptist, c. 1660-1670.

Oil on canvas. 39 x 50 cm.

226. Claude Lorrain
Pastoral Landscape with a Flight into Egypt, 1663.

Oil on canvas. 193 x 147 cm.

16-18 18th-Century Italian Painting

Italy's artistic supremacy now passed to France. However, a visit to Italy continued to be considered obligatory for artists and aristocrats from all over Europe. Its main cities were thus ideal scenes for the cultivation of the new aesthetic currents stimulated by interest in the Classical ruins, archaeology and the rise of collecting in Europe.

The centres of creation continued to be Rome, Naples and Venice, the latter city shining forth as a particular focus of innovation. Giambattista Tiepolo (1696-1770), one of the most important artists of the century was born there. *The Death of Hyacinthus* (Cat. 394), considered one of his masterpieces, illustrates a mythological theme from Ovid's *Metamorphosis*. The painting displays the most characteristic notes of his style: the richness of the colouring, which is combined with a very personal palette in which cold, pale tones predominate, the monumentality of the figures and finally the virtuosity and scenic efficacy of the composition. A painter endowed with great talent, he was in demand as a frescoist to decorate the ceilings of the palaces of the principle courts of Europe, including the Royal Palace in Madrid, the city in which he died in 1770.

Only fourteen years older than his pupil, Tiepolo's master, Giovanni Battista Piazzetta (1683-1754), developed an intensely personal style. In his *Portrait of Giulia Lama* (Cat. 316), a poetess, painter and also his pupil, he combined the vigorous chiaroscuro and low colour range of the Caravaggist tradition with the delicacy and intimacy demanded by the new tastes of the 18th century.

In addition to the continuation of this Baroque current from the previous century, 18th-century Venice also witnessed the development of a new genre based on views of the city and its architecture, the *vedute*. Although the precedents of this style lie in Dutch painting, for instance in Berckheyde (see room 25), two cultural tendencies of the period influenced its development in Italy: interest in the architecture of Classical antiquity and the development of stage settings, which began at the end of the 17th century. The complex idealised architecture of the two paintings by the Roman painter and architect Giovanni Panini (c. 1691-1765) illustrate this tendency in 18th-century taste (Cat. 311 and 312).

However, the genre soon evolved towards the representation of architectural scenes from real cities. The interest of foreign clients, especially English ones, who wished to hang souvenirs of their 'Grand Tour' of Italy in their homes, was undoubtedly decisive in this evolution.

394. **Giambattista Tiepolo**
The Death of Hyacinthus, 1752-1753.

Oil on canvas. 287 x 232 cm.

The first master of the genre was Canaletto (1697-1768), a painter who was trained within the scenographic tradition and who was able, perhaps better than anyone, to capture the magic and charm of Venice and its canals in his paintings. The *Piazza San Marco in Venice* (Cat. 75) and the *View of the Canal Grande from San Vio* (Cat. 76) portray two characteristic views of Venice, executed with all the skill in perspective and the precision so characteristic of the artist's colouring. Although thronging with human activity, these paintings are essentially dominated by the architecture and light of the city.

The works of Bernardo Bellotto (1720-1780), nephew of Canaletto, and Francesco Guardi (1712-1793), brother-in-law of Giambattista Tiepolo, display less topographic rigour and more poetic liberty. Bellotto worked in various cities of Italy and Germany before settling at the court of Stanislas Augustus Poniatowski, king of Poland. The beautiful idealised view, or *capriccio* seen here (Cat.

76. **Canaletto**
View of Canal Grande from San Vio, Venice, before 1723.

Oil on canvas. 140.5 x 204.5 cm.

75. **Canaletto**
View of Piazza San Marco, Venice, before 1723.

Oil on canvas. 141.5 x 204.5 cm.

40) is from his Italian period. Venice was almost the sole subject of Francesco Guardi's many paintings. The *Canal Grande with S. Simeone Piccolo and Sta Lucia* (Cat. 175) and its companion painting (Cat. 174) display the city's main artery from two different viewpoints. The free brushwork creates a wide spectrum of atmospheric effects based on a rigorous study of the light. The work of the two artists forms a prelude to the artistic tastes of the following century. While the luminous composition of Bellotto makes us think of the delicate and serene Italian landscapes of Corot, the moist, palpitating light of Guardi's Venice anticipates that of Impressionism in the last third of the 19th century.

The panorama of 18th-century Venetian painting also includes a genre which, despite dating from the previous century, was particularly valued by Enlightenment taste for its reaction against the rhetoric of Baroque. This was genre painting. Its greatest exponent in Venice was Pietro Falca (1702-1785), known as Pietro Longhi,

whose works, which are generally small in format, portray the habits of the bourgeoisie and aristocracy of Venice with a constant attention to significant detail and an unparalleled ability to evoke atmosphere. *The Tickle* (Cat. 224) allows us a glimpse into the privacy of a family scene in the room of a Venetian palace. The elegance of the restricted palette with its green hues and the lightness of the brushwork, which evokes French Rococo, do not conceal the sense of restlessness emanating from the painting. This delicate but almost Rousseauian sentimentality is not totally foreign to the great storms of passion that would invade Europe with Romanticism at the beginning of the following century.

175. **Francesco Guardi**
View of Canal Grande with San Simeone Piccolo and Santa Lucia, c.1780.

Oil on canvas. 48 x 78 cm.

224. **Pietro Longhi**
The Tickle, c. 1755.

Oil on canvas. 61 x 48 cm.

19 17th-Century Flemish Painting

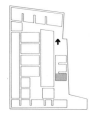

The conflict between the Spanish monarchy and the Protestant world brought about the gradual separation of the northern provinces of the Netherlands from Flanders, a process which affected painting and cultural life in general during the first third of the 17th century. While Flanders continued to look towards Italy, Dutch painting began to explore other paths (see Rooms 20 to 27).

The blossoming of Flemish painting during this period was primarily due to Rubens (1577-1640). As with other early Baroque artists, his style involved a break with Mannerism and a return to the first half of the 16th century. In his work the rich colours and technical fluency of the Flemish tradition are synthesised with the Italian models, especially the figures and compositions of the late Michelangelo and the manner of constructing space through colour of Titian. It is precisely in Rubens' copies of paintings by Titian that his capacity for transcending the conventions of his time is best seen. One of these is the *The Toilet of Venus* (Cat. 350) exhibited here, a composition in which Titian tackled a recurrent theme of Neo-Platonic philosophy (ideal beauty manifested in the mirror of love), with which Rubens must have been familiar. In addition to this composition, Rubens is represented in this room by two sketches (one of which, *The Blinding of Samson*, (Cat. 351) merits attention for its splendid drawing) and a portrait. The prototype for the *Portrait of a Young Woman with a Rosary* (Cat. 352) comes from a tradition long established in Flanders, as can be seen by comparing it with the *Portrait of Giovanni Battista di Castaldo* (Cat. 291) painted half a century before by Anthonis Mor (1591-1576). The crimson drapery filling the background constitutes a peculiar archaism, but executed with Rubens' characteristic brilliance it adds power to the vivacity of the expression and the smoothness of the brushwork in the figure.

The *Portrait of Jacques Le Roy* (Cat. 135), which Van Dyck (1599-1641) painted in Antwerp in 1631 shortly before his last period in England, is the sole, albeit splendid, work in the Museum by one of the most acclaimed portraitists in the history of painting .

Despite the above-mentioned divergence between Dutch and Flemish painting, the genre painting so characteristic of the Dutch school was also cultivated in Flanders. This was also the case with the still life and the landscape. Most of the Flemish examples of these genres have been hung with the Dutch for reasons of visual

350. Peter Paul Rubens
The Toilet of Venus, after 1629.

Oil on canvas. 137 x 111 cm.

coherence. However, an exception has been made for four early landscapes which add to the panorama of Flemish painting in this room.

It is possible that Jan Brueghel the Elder (1568-1625) painted the small oil on copper depicting *Christ in the Storm on the Sea of Galilee* (Cat. 66) in Milan. However, it must still be looked upon as one of the last examples of the interesting tradition of ideal landscapes cultivated so successfully in Flanders in the 16th century. The richness of the colouring and the technique which won the artist the nickname of 'Velvet' Brueghel are easier to appreciate in *The Garden of Eden* (Cat. A.801). There is good reason to suppose that the version exhibited here is the first of a series of variants scattered in different collections. The friendship between Rubens and Jan Brueghel the Elder is well known, as are their occasional artistic collaborations. They both signed a panel depicting Adam and Eve in the Garden of Eden now in the Mauritshuis of the Hague. It is therefore not surprising that some of the animals that can be seen in the painting we see here, including the horse and the pair of lions on the left and the tigers on the right, are derived from prototypes established by Rubens.

The beautiful pair of landscapes attributed to the artist we call the 'Monogrammist 'IDM' (probably an artist from the circle of Joos de Momper, whose work is now being revised by the experts) (Cat. 288 and 289) follow a scheme of composition of which the first versions are found in the work of Jan Brueghel the Elder. They reflect a taste for the Italian which became widespread in the Netherlands and which constitutes the theme of Room 20.

135. Anthony van Dyck
Portrait of Jacques Le Roy, 1631.

Oil on canvas. 117.8 x 100.6 cm.

20-21 17th-Century Dutch Painting: Italianate Currents and Portraits

The Dutch painting of the 17th century first received widespread international attention due to the interest of enlightened French and English critics, especially the Pre-Romantics, during the following century. The Pre-Romantic critics characterised Dutch painting in contrast to the Classicism they identified with Italian painting, establishing polar contrasts such as realism as opposed to idealism, sentimentality as opposed to formalism, and worldly as opposed to religious themes. The historians of the 19th century then gave these characteristics internal coherence, explaining them as manifestations of the national spirit which had led the Dutch people to rebel and gain its independence.

Current historiography rejects the two stereotypes and even tends to diminish the habitual distinction between Dutch and Flemish painting. Although it must be approached with caution, this reaction amongst contemporary historians provides us with a better means of understanding and appreciating artists such as Honthorst and Sweerts who were marginalised by the Romantic critics due to their being situated midway between the pictorial cultures of Italy and Holland.

It was decided when planning the lay-out of the Museum that this Italian-influenced Dutch painting should be located next to the rooms devoted to Rubens and his time. A similar wish to avoid excessive contrasts led to placing a room devoted solely to the portrait after it to act as a transitional area.

The most important case of Italian influence in Dutch painting is the diffusion of Caravaggism. Naturalism, the depiction of actions caught at a dramatic moment, and a colouring and chiaroscuro conditioned by focal lighting were imported from Italy in the 1620s and became an integral feature of Dutch painting. The main centre of diffusion was Utrecht, the city which was to be the home, after their stays in Italy, of Dirk J. van Baburen (c. 1595-1624), whose *St Sebastian Tended by St Irene* (Cat. 347) is exhibited in Room 12 due to its stylistic proximity to the painting of Rome, and Gerrit van Honthorst (1592-1656), whose *Happy Violinist* (Cat. 194) is exhibited in Room 22 due to its influence on the development of Dutch genre painting. In Room 20 we see two intermediate examples: *Esau Selling his Birthright* (Cat. 393) by Hendrik Terbrugghen (1588?-1629), another painter who lived in Utrecht after his journey to Italy, displays a personal pictorial language nonetheless close to Honthorst's. *The Supper at Emmaus* (Cat. 375)

375. Matthias Stom
The Supper at Emmaus, c. 1633-1639.

Oil on canvas. 111.8 x 152.4 cm.

393. Hendrick ter Brugghen
Esau Selling His Birthright, c. 1627.

Oil on canvas. 106.7 x 138.8 cm.

17th-Century Dutch Painting: Italianate Currents and Portraits

by Matthias Stom (c. 1600-c. 1650), an artist who spent a great part of his career in Italy, represents a more stereotyped assimilation of Caravaggism.

The work of Bartholomeus Breenbergh reflects another type of Italian influence. The drawings of antique ruins he did in Rome during the 1620s were to be the basis of a long career specialising in ideal landscapes, such as the one exhibited here (Cat. 62). More interesting is the career of M. Sweerts (1624-1664), a Flemish painter born in Brussels in 1624. His painting *Soldiers Playing Dice* (Cat. 384) connects with the genre painting which Dutch painters of the previous generation, such as Pieter van Laer (c. 1592-1642), had cultivated in Italy. The extraordinary *Boy in a Turban* (Cat. 385) painted circa 1655 is a late but brilliant and highly personal interpretation of Caravaggist manners and themes.

Gerard Terborch (1617-1682) was one of the last important Dutch artists to go to Italy. His *Portrait of a Man Reading* (Cat. 392) is an example of the tendency initiated by Rembrandt of presenting the subject against an everyday background. This aim is served admirably by the treatment of the light and the painter's refined use of colour. The portraits other than those of Terborch and Nicolaes Maes (1634-1693) displayed in Room 21 can be divided into two groups. One of them includes, along with a portrait long attributed to Rembrandt (Cat. 331), their contemporaries or followers, such as Thomas H. de Keyser (1596/97-1667) (Cat. 209), Govert Flinck (1615-1650) (Cat. 143), Ferdinand Bol (1616-1680) (Cat. 51) and Bartholomeus van der Helst (1613?-1670) (Cat. 184). The other, containing Caspar Netscher (c. 1635/36-1684) (Cat. 301 and 302) and Frans van Mieris (1635-1681) (Cat. 286) displays a notable change in taste. In the last decades of the century Dutch painting lost something of its unique character as it came closer to the international Classicism emanating from France.

392. Gerard ter Borch
Portrait of a Man Reading a Coranto, c. 1675.

Oil on canvas. 48 x 39.5 cm.

FIRST FLOOR

22-26 17th-Century Dutch Painting: Scenes from Everyday Life, Interiors and Landscapes

These five rooms contain an uninterrupted series of paintings depicting scenes from everyday life, interiors, architectural views and townscapes, landscapes and seascapes. Although they were also cultivated elsewhere, these genres have always been associated with the history of Dutch painting and seen as its distinctive features.

Large full-length group portraits such as the *Family Group in a Landscape* (Cat. 179) by Frans Hals (1582 or 1583-1666) are also associated with Dutch painting. The skill of the brushwork and the vivacity and psychological immediacy of the personages are characteristic features of his style. Because of these qualities, he was held in esteem by his contemporaries until the mid-17th century, when tastes changed towards a preference for more polished works. Hals was forgotten for two hundred years. In the second half of the 19th century, the influence of literary and pictorial realism led to a reappraisal of Hals, and his style left a deep mark on that of the great precursors of modern painting, from Courbet to Whistler and Manet to Van Gogh.

Although idiosyncratic, Hals's style did not lack precedents. The nearest was the influence of the Utrecht Caravaggisti. If we compare the *Happy Violinist* (Cat. 194) by Gerrit van Honthorst (1590-1656) or the *Young Man Playing a Lute* (Cat. 73) attributed to Jan van Bijlert (1603-1676) to the works of Hals, it is possible to discern the same exploitation of the theatrical effects in the fleeting expressions and gestures (the gazes, the hands, or the movement of the dog which is pressing against the dress of the girl in the family group). Important differences can also be seen, especially in Hals's light and natural perspective, which contrast with the focal lighting and forced perspective of the Caravaggisti.

With these stylistic changes which led him away from Caravaggism, Hals contributed in defining the new course of Dutch painting of scenes from everyday life. Nineteenth-century critics, who considered this kind of painting to be the vital expression of the Dutch national genius, saw it as a break with Classicism and a precursor to modern realism. We now know that it is not difficult to fit it into the doctrinal framework of Classicism as it was understood in the 16th and 17th centuries in both Holland and Italy. The distinction between the genres of tragedy and comedy, which originated in Classical times, justified certain 'low' forms of artistic expression suitable for describing the characteristic features of reality. In this field, that of comedy in the theatre, the artist could

179. Frans Hals
Family Group in a Landscape, c. 1645-1648.

Oil on canvas. 202 x 285 cm.

disregard idealisation and the formal rules demanded by the 'high'; forms of expression. The respective equivalents of this hierarchy in the art of painting were, on the one hand, the representation of religious or mythological 'histories' and, on the other, of genre scenes. Despite this, although the painting of 'histories' never ceased to be cultivated in Holland, the importance of what ended up being described as 'genre painting' marks an important difference from Italian and international Classicism. Its importance contributed to the tendency towards different stylistic formulae in 17th-century Dutch painting.

A point of no return in this differential tendency in Dutch genre painting might have been reached in the work of Adriaen Brouwer (1605–1638), a Flemish painter who worked in Hals's workshop.

17th-Century Dutch Painting: Scenes from Everyday Life, Interiors and Landscapes

Village Scene with Men Drinking (Cat. 65) illustrates the effects of wine drinking. The subject, viewed from the satirical, moralising manner of popular proverbs, falls within a Flemish tradition which had been cultivated in the 16th century by Pieter Brueghel the Elder. The novelty consisted in the method of painting: the spontaneity in the composition of the scene, the earthy colours and the brushwork, which appear to be the equivalent of painting of the almost caricatural line of genre engravings.

After having lived in Holland (Haarlem and Amsterdam), Brouwer settled in Antwerp. His painting was a point of departure for David Teniers II (1610-1680), another Flemish artist whose enormous output contributed to the spreading of genre painting to Catholic countries, especially France and Spain. His brushstroke is

195. **Pieter Hendricksz de Hooch**
Woman with Needlework and a Child, c. 1662-1668.

Oil on canvas. 54.6 x 45.1 cm.

241. **Nicolaes Maes**
The Naughty Drummer, c. 1655.

Oil on canvas. 62 x 66.4 cm.

tighter than that of Brouwer and although his colour range is also narrow, the painter allows himself to include isolated touches of crimsons, blues and greens. The main reason for his success lies in his capacity to compose interesting, varied scenes (Cat. 386 and 387). With his work and that of his Dutch contemporaries, Adriaen van Ostade (1610-1685) (Cat. 306) and Gerrit Dou (1613-1675) (Cat. 132) genre painting became established and expanded to satisfy a growing demand. This was accompanied by a process of stylistic consolidation: the invention of compositional formulae which could be repeated with variants and the establishment of a gentler and more conventional pictorial language. This evolution was accentuated in the work of artists from the following generation, whose members included Gabriel Metsu (1629-1667) (Cat. 285), Jackob Ochtervelt (1634-1682) (Cat. 304) and Jan Steen (1625 or 1626-1679). Steen's paintings contain frequent references to theatrical characters and situations, as in the presumed *Self-Portrait*

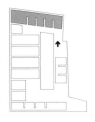

(Cat. 373), which presents us with a personage dressed (archaically) in actor's clothing, and the *Tavern Scene* (Cat. A 826), which appears to be extracted from a *comedia dell'arte* situation: a pimp offering a pregnant woman to an old man absorbed in the pleasure of lighting his pipe.

At the same time, an important innovation arose: the type of genre painting sometimes called Intimisme and practised mainly by artists such as Gerard Terborch, Pieter de Hooch and especially Jan Vermeer. Although contemporaries continued to see in it allegorical meanings, such as the opposition between the active life and the contemplative life, the dependence of this painting on literature or drama declined, giving way to a more direct interest in domestic life and a greater concern for purely pictorial problems. *Portrait of a Man Reading a Coranto* by Gerard ter Borch (Cat. 390, Room 21), which we decided to group with the portraits, is close to this genre, and *The Naughty Drummer* (Cat. 241) by Nicolaes Maes (1634-1693) is a good example of it. However, the artist who best represents it here is Pieter de Hooch (1629-1684). In *Woman with Needlework and a Child* (Cat. 195) Hooch concentrates on the treatment of light and the ordering of space by means of a succession of receding frontal planes. The same pictorial concerns seem to be the main inspiration for the *Interior of the Burgomaster's Chamber in the Amsterdam Town Hall* (Cat. 196). The artist has resorted to difficult plays on perspective (for example, the extremely wide angle of vision) with the aim of accentuating the spectator's sensation of being in the hall. The treatment of colour is directed towards achieving the same effect. As for the figures, they appear to have been painted merely to provide scale and consistency to the space.

When Hooch arrived in Amsterdam, Emanuel de Witte (1617-1692) was the painter enjoying the greatest fame there as a specialist in architectural interiors (Cat. 439). But the principal Dutch master in the genre was Pieter Saenredam (1597-1665), who worked in Haarlem. His style could be described as a combination in equal parts of meticulousness and poetic inspiration. He used his deep knowledge of the rules of perspective and architecture expressively, resorting to distortions subtly cloaked with objectivity. A contemporary of the Caravaggisti, like them Saenredam was a painter of light, although for opposing reasons. The *West Front of the Mariakerk, Utrecht* (Cat. 362) is one of his few paintings

362. **Pieter Jansz Saenredam**
The West Front of the Mariakerk, Utrecht, 1662.

Oil on oak panel. 65.1 x 51.2 cm.

representing the exterior of a building. A mosaic of grey, silvery and golden brushsrokes, with the occasional touch of pink, greenish yellow and leaden blue describe the incidence of the soft light of a Dutch midday on the ashlars of the medieval building.

17th-Century Dutch Painting: Scenes from Everyday Life, Interiors and Landscapes

Passing from architectural views and townscapes to landscapes, we observe the same specifically Dutch evolution which, along with genre painting, constitutes its other great differential feature.

The course of this evolution can be seen by comparing the *Mountain Landscape with Castle* (Cat. 365) by Roelandt Savery (1576-1639) painted in 1609, the *Extensive Landscape with Armed Men* (Cat. 370) by Hercules Segers (1589-1633) painted circa 1630 and the *View of Naarden* (Cat. 354) by Jacob van Ruisdael (1628-1684) painted in 1647. Although he was Dutch, Savery was working in Prague in the service of Rudolph II when he painted *Mountain Landscape*. The literary and imaginary qualities of its appearance are better understood in the context of the late Mannerist taste dominating the Imperial court. However, the painting was probably composed from sketches taken from nature by the artist in the Tyrol. Segers' work is also an imaginary composition, but its literary connotations are less important. The scheme of composition with a plane fading into a distant horizon, framed by a foreground of trees and low hills, is an invention of his which was adopted by

370. **Hercules Pietersz Seghers**
Extensive Landscape with Armed Men, c.1625-1635.

Oil on canvas. 36.5 x 54.3 cm.

354. Jacob Isaacksz van Ruisdael
View of Naarden, 1647.

Oil on oak panel. 34.8 x 67 cm.

many of his contemporaries for the technical challenge involved. The problem was how to give the painting the sensation of space without using linear perspective. Segers achieves this partly through colour and largely through the groups of buildings and trees which help to establish successive planes of depth. In the case of Ruisdael's work, we find ourselves before a real landscape familiar to its contemporaries. The effect of depth is achieved almost exclusively by the gradation of colour and the alternating planes of sun and shade which finally fade into the horizon.

The qualities of Dutch landscapism most admired by the Impressionists, the simplicity and spontaneity of vision and the faithful depiction of light, were achieved at the end of the 1630s with the maturing of the styles of the artists born around 1600. Jan van Goyen (1596-1656) and Salomon van Ruysdael (1600-1670), the uncle of Jacob, belong to this generation. Van Goyen's *Winter Landscape with Figures on Ice* (Cat. 167) illustrates his characteristic, almost monochrome, manner. The literary connotations of the subject (the seasons and their respective tasks) are less important than the problem of depicting the space and the winter light.

Meindert Hobbema (1638-1709) and Aelbert Cuyp (1620-1691) are, along with the aforementioned Jacob van Ruisdael, the most outstanding figures of the second generation of landscapists. *Evening Landscape* (Cat. 117) by Cuyp combines foreign topographical motifs (the rocky massif on the horizon) with

a crepuscular light like that of Claude Lorrain and a tonal colouring of typically Dutch conception.

The interdependence of light, colour and pictorial space, which was definitely the major contribution of Dutch landscapism to the history of painting, lends itself to an especially subtle treatment in seascapes, where the line of the horizon is defined by the meeting of the sky and water. Although *View of Alkmaar* (Cat. 793) painted by Salomon van Ruysdael depicts a fluvial environment, the evocation of space through the tonal modulation of blues, whites and greys could be used to illustrate the highest pictorial values of the seascape. The work is a prodigy of beauty, simplicity, calm and transparency. That of his nephew Jacob, *Rough Sea with Sailing Vessels* (Cat. 359), explores the contrast between the darkness of the turbulent waves and the whiteness of their spray under the light of the storm. This was probably the painting that John M. W. Turner saw a century and a half later in a London collection and from which, according to his biographer Cunningham, he drew the inspiration for his own rough sea which he presented at the Royal Academy exhibition of 1827 under the title of *Port Ruysdael*.

117. **Aelbert Jacobsz Cuyp**
Evening Landscape, after 1645.

Oil on oak panel. 48.3 x 74.9 cm.

793. Salomon Jacobsz van Ruysdael
View of Alkmaar From the Sea, c. 1650.

Oil on oak panel. 36 x 32.5 cm.

27 17th-Century Still Lifes

The still life developed greatly as of the end of the 16th century. Although it was also cultivated in Italy, France, and Spain, it has traditionally been considered a typically Dutch genre. The Calvinist rejection of religious art was said to have led to painting interested exclusively in depicting the appearance of things and in technical questions. The still life was a lesson in observation and painting. In opposition to this explanation, recent historiography has underlined its symbolic functions. The most important case is said to be the symbolism of the so-called 'vanities'. Thus, the open watch which can be seen in the paintings of Kalf (1619-1693) (Cat. 202 and 204) or the broken cup in Heda's composition (1593-1680) (Cat. 181) can be seen as representing the proximity of death. The caterpillars and butterflies of the flower pieces could allude to the devouring action of time.

The still lifes with flowers also lead us towards other meanings. The rare species that A. Bosschaert (1573-1621) selected for the *Chinese Vase with Flowers* must be understood in the light of his clientele's interest in the natural sciences. The painting is a sort of botanic portrait for scientists and amateur scientists.

Seventeenth-century Holland saw a rise in collections not only of flowers but also of Chinese porcelain, carpets and gold or silverwork. And, naturally, of paintings. The fact that a painting could go beyond being simply a portrait in a collection to become a collectable work in itself gives rise to interesting speculations. In Kalf's epitaph, composed by the poet Van der Hoeven, it is confirmed that the artist knew how to paint the richest treasures, but that no treasure could reward his worth.

We thus return to the traditional interpretation: the still life is a lesson in seeing and painting. But this does not contradict its symbolic interpretations. In a brief text on the 'vanities' André Chastel compared the table on which the objects of the still life are arranged with a sacrificial altar: the more capable the painter is of capturing the freshness of the petals, the softness of the materials, and the diversity of the reflections in liquids and metals, the more dramaticly and effectively he achieves his goal of denouncing the vanity of appearances.

181. Willem Claesz Heda

Still Life with Rummer, Silver Tazza, Pie and other Objects, 1634.

Oil on oak panel. 43.7 x 68.2 cm.

180. Juan van der Hamen y Leon

Still Life with porcelain and sweets, c. 1627.

Oil on canvas. 77 x 100 cm.

28 From Rococo to Neoclassicism

The symptoms of a profound crisis in European culture become apparent at the turn of the 18th century. One of the consequences of this was a change in tastes which brought into question the Classical values defended by the Academy—the primacy of drawing and composition, aesthetic idealism, and the hierarchy of the forms of expression. Instead of seeking to uplift or morally edify the onlooker, the work of art was to appeal to the feelings and to gratify. It is significant that the new taste, which passed into history with the derogatory name of Rococo, originated precisely in the fields of decoration and genre painting.

Rococo rapidly spread from France to the rest of Europe thanks to the growing internationalisation of aristocratic habits. This same network of diffusion, so characteristic of the 18th century, allowed a new taste to spread in the mid-century as a reaction to Rococo: Neoclassicism. Despite its restorative nature, Neoclassicism is not a simple phenomenon; if it defended academic values, it did so to search moral and rational foundations for artistic activity. Allied with the Encyclopaedists, its development forms part of the complex history of the Enlightenment. At the end of the century it became associated with the French Revolution, but also with anti-revolutionary tendencies (e.g. in England) and in many places with the first wave of Romanticism.

The first of the great painters of Rococo is Antoine Watteau (1684-1721). The Museum possesses two of his works. *The Rest* (Cat. 431) forms part of a series of military scenes painted by the artist in his youth. *Pierrot Content* (Cat. 432) depicts a garden scene with characters dressed in costumes from the *comedia dell'arte*; its subject matter links it to the series known as *fêtes gallantes*, which includes the work for which he was admitted to the Academy, the celebrated *Pilgrimage to the Island of Cythera*. Inspired by Rubens and Titian, whom he admired and studied in the Parisian collections, Watteau's pictorial style is deeply innovative and personal. Nicolas Lancret (1690-1743), by whom there are two works in the Museum (Cat. 215 and 216), and Jean-Baptiste Joseph Pater (1695-1736), whose *Concert Champêtre* (Cat. 313) is presented here, were followers of his in terms of style, and especially in terms of subject matter.

The best exponent of Rococo taste is perhaps François Boucher (1703-1770), who received the patronage of Madame Pompadour. The scenes from his paintings, painted in bright and pleasant colours,

432. Jean Antoine Watteau
Pierrot Content, c. 1712.

Oil on canvas. 35 x 31 cm.

appealed directly to the collective imagination of his large clientele. *La Toilette* (Cat. 58) is one of his most characteristic and greatest works.

The case of Jean-Baptiste Chardin (1699-1779) is a good example of the cultural complexity of the 18th century. Despite the stylistic coherence of his painting, he was appreciated for the most diverse reasons by opposing sides. A follower of the Dutch fashion which spread in France at the same time as the Rococo, he was nonetheless admitted to the Academy in 1728 precisely for his still lifes. He later became one of the artists preferred by the

Encyclopaedists. The Museum has three still lifes by Chardin, all three from 1728. *Still Life with Jug and Copper Cauldron* (Cat. 118) is exhibited in Room 27 along with Dutch painting of the previous century. *Still Life with Cat and Rayfish* (cat. 120) and its companion painting (Cat. 119), works which reveal the pictorial qualities praised by Diderot, are displayed in this room.

Jean-Honoré Fragonard (1732-1806) and Hubert Robert (1733-1808) met while studying at the Academy in Rome at the beginning of the 1760s, a time when Italian models were becoming a point of reference for French taste once more. Robert finally opted for Classical landscape painting, as can be seen in his *Interior of the Temple of Diana* (Cat. 343). Fragonard, who had little interest in the Academy and official commissions, returned to the Rococo style and introduced important renovations to it with his personal development of the Venetian tradition. *The See-saw* (Cat. 148) is a forerunner of his celebrated work *The Swing*, which is kept in the Wallace Collection in London. Both were commissioned by the same client, the Baron de St Julien. In the *Portrait of Mademoiselle Duthé* (Cat. A 805) we can appreciate the subtlety of colour and agility of brushstroke characteristic of his mature style.

England was the scene of unprecedented artistic and cultural splendour during this century. In the field of painting the portrait acquired notable importance. Reynolds and Gainsborough, with their diametrically opposed concepts of painting, provided the genre with its main models.

Sir Joshua Reynolds (1723-1792), founder of the Royal Academy of Arts, was one of the century's most important theorists. He created an eclectic style from his study of the artistic classics which can be considered one of the best formulations of Neoclassicism in European painting. The *Portrait of Frances, Countess of Dartmouth* (Cat. 334), a work from his early period, is reminiscent of Van Dyck. Thomas Gainsborough (1727-1788), the other great personality of the 18th century in England had a free brushstroke and luminous colouring. In his portrait of *Miss Sara Buxton* (Cat. 153), the artist attempted to express the personality and mood of the sitter through the clothing, the landscape and the dominant tones of the painting.

120. Jean Baptiste Simeon Chardin
Still-Life With Cat and Rayfish, c. 1728.

Oil on canvas. 79.5 x 63 cm.

29-30 19th-Century American Painting

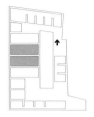

Rooms 29 and 30 offer the public a vision of 19th-century American painting. The paintings assembled here represent a chapter in the history of art largely absent from European museums.

19th-century American painting began to acquire the characteristics of a national school with its peculiar assimilation of Romanticism during the first years of independence. Before independence, the art of what was still a colonial society had been under strong British influence. The most outstanding artist was John Singleton Copley (1738-1815), whose portraits, which are characterised by very precise draughtsmanship, conserve the appearance of some of the leading figures of the time. The Museum has three works from his American period: the *Portrait of Judge Martin Howard*, 1767, (Cat. 99), the *Portrait of Mrs Samuel Hill (Miriam Kilby)*, circa 1764, (Cat. 98) and *Mrs Joshua Henshaw II (Catherine Hill)*, circa 1772, (Cat. 97). The most outstanding of his followers was Charles Wilson Peale (1741-1827), whose portrait of *Isabella and John Stewart*, circa 1775 (Cat. 315) continues the tradition of 18th-century European painting.

After independence, the landscape was to prove the favoured vehicle of expression for the new nationalistic and romantic inspirations. In an atmosphere of relative isolation from European art, American landscape painting, the main movement in which was the Hudson River School, was characterised by an exaltation of nature arising from an attitude which saw the American landscape as a new Garden of Eden, a virgin territory given to the pioneers as a reward for their efforts.

The founder of the Hudson River School was Thomas Cole (1801-1848), a painter and engraver born in England. His *Expulsion—Moon and Firelight* (Cat. 95) and *Cross at Sunset* (Cat. 96) are examples of a symbolic and spiritual tendency which has its English counterpart in the followers of Turner. The followers of Cole included Church, his only pupil, and other painters such as Durand, Kensett, Cropsey and Bierstadt, all represented in the Museum, who prolong the Romantic landscape tradition over the course of the 19th century.

Another tendency developed alongside the Romantic school, that of the painters known as the Luminists, whose approach to landscape was more lyrical and less theatrical. These painters, the most outstanding of whom were Martin Johnson Heade (1819-1904) and Fitz Lane (1804-1865), usually painted seascapes and coastal

91. James Goodwyn Clonney
Fishing Party on Long Island Sound Off New Rochelle, 1847.

Oil on canvas. 66 x 92.7 cm.

95. Thomas Cole
Expulsion. Moon and Firelight, c. 1828.

Oil on canvas. 91.4 x 122 cm.

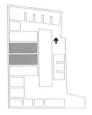

landscapes from the East Coast, such as *Spouting Rock* (Cat. 577), by the former and *Ten Pound Island, Gloucester, Massachusetts* (Cat. 635), by the latter.

Parallel to the development of landscapism there appeared the specifically American tendency of genre painting, which contained two major facets: the first dealt with the representation of scenes from everyday life, as in the painting by James G. Clonney (1812-1867) *Fishing Party on Long Island Sound off New Rochelle* (Cat. 91), which was painted before the Civil War and can be looked upon as an idyllic image of American society in the early 19th century. The second facet was ethnological in inspiration and involved the painting of Indian scenes, largely constituting a projection of adventure fantasies concerning the conquest and colonisation of the West. It undergoes an evolution lasting from the 1840s to the first decades of the 20th century. At first the artists painted scenes they could have seen themselves. This is the case, for example, of the painting of George Catlin *The Falls of St Anthony* (Cat. 487). After the Civil War, with the modernisation of American society, the 'Indian scenes' increasingly became stereotypes of collective fantasy, as in the nocturnal scene by Frederick Remington (1861-1909) *Apache Fire Signal* (Cat. 722).

Another distinct characteristic of American painting was the development of a particular kind of still life cultivated in the last decades of the 19th century and the beginning of the 20th characterised by the detailed depiction of reality using the illusionistic effects of *trompe l'oeil*. The Museum contains paintings by the leading exponents of this genre, William M. Harnett (1848-1892) and John F. Peto (1854-1907). In his works, such as *Materials for a Leisure Hour* (Cat. 574), Harnett presents everyday objects (a pipe, book, newspaper, mug, bottle and matches) painted with great solidity and arranged in a perfectly balanced and studied composition. His follower Peto would take this tradition to its limits, as we see in *Tom's River* (Cat. 700), a work in which he uses elements of theatrical illusionism—the painting of the frame to make it a continuation of the painting, the hanging string, the shadows of the nails, the scraps of torn paper, the incised letters—which end up giving the overall arrangement a surprising air of unreality.

The naturalist or realist tendency was developed during the last third of the century when American artists turned their attention back towards Europe. The outstanding figure is that of Winslow Homer

700. **John Frederick Peto**
Tom's River, 1905.

Oil on canvas. 50.8 x 40.6 cm.

(1836-1910), whose painting is an American equivalent of Courbet and the Barbizon School, although his style is independent of French painting (see *Waverly Oaks* Cat. 589). In 1883 he went to live in Prout's Neck, Maine, and his works reflect the hard life of the fishermen, the power of the sea and the heroism of man in his struggle against the elements. *The Signal of Distress* of 1890 (Cat. 588) belongs to this period.

James A. Whistler (1834-1906) was an artist from the same generation as Homer, but situated at the opposite extreme. He was the typical uprooted American painter, living in Europe and working in London and Paris, never returning to the United States. His taste for Japanese art led him to adopt simplicity in composition and colouring. As from 1870 he devoted more time to the portrait: his *Pink and Gold. The Neapolitan* (Cat. 784) is an example of his skillful brushwork and his refined treatment of colour. The influence of Impressionism (especially Monet) and Japanese art are also evident in the works on display by William Merrit Chase (1849-1916) *Shinnecock Hills* (Cat. A.835) and *The Kimono* (Cat. 501).

Finally, we come to the works of a painter who, despite being born in Florence to American parents, is not considered completely American, since he passed long periods in Venice, Paris, London and other European cities. This is John Singer Sargent (1856-1925), a painter who admired the painting of Velázquez and Frans Hals and who was influenced by Impressionism. The *Venetian Onion Seller* (Cat. 731) is from his Venetian period, a painting notable for its free brushwork and its interest in the problems of light. It reveals the closeness of Sargent's style and that of the Spaniard Sorolla, with whom he had a close friendship. Sargent attained great fame as a portraitist of the British and American aristocracy due to the skill of his brushwork and the elegance he was able to infuse into his personages. The *Portrait of Millicent, Duchess of Sutherland* (Cat. 732) characteristically illustrates this aspect of his work.

589. Winslow Homer
Waverly Oaks, 1864.

Oil on paper on panel. 33.6 x 25.4 cm.

We look back on 19th-century art through a critical filter which reveals to us more than anything the roots of modernism. Our attention therefore focuses on impressionism, as the initial period of modern art, and the movements seen as leading up to it over de course of the century: the anti-Classicist rebellion of Romanticism and Realism, and the realist doctrine that circumscribed pictorial expression to the domain of the visual senses.

The partisan critical nature of this scheme must not lead us to reject it as invalid. The history of art abounds in similar schemes, beginning with Vasari, who explained the art of the 14th and 15th centuries as a prelude to the Renaissance of the 16th century.

Whatever the case, if we accept the explanation which links the art of the Enlightenment with that of the 20th century via Romanticism, Realism and Impressionism, no artist could stand as a better source and guide for it than Goya (1746-1828). The three paintings in the Museum belong to the painter's mature period. His portrait of *Asensio Juliá in his Studio* (Cat. 166) stands out for its delicacy and audacity. Goya dedicated it to a painter, a pupil and friend of his, on the occasion of his collaboration in the frescoes for San Antonio de la Florida. *El Tío Paquete* (Cat. 165), produced in the same period as the *Pinturas Negras*, or 'Black Paintings', was painted shortly before Goya went into exile in Bordeaux, where he passed his final years.

Although Theodore Gericault (1791-1824) was associated with the beginnings of Romanticism in France, his painting deliberately evokes the monumentality of the Classical models of the Italian Renaissance and antique sculpture. *Horse Race* (Cat. 157) is a good example of this. In contrast, the two small oils by Delacroix (1798-1863) (Cat. 126 and 127) are fully Romantic in conception and execution.

Caspar David Friedrich (1774-1840) is the main representative of German Romanticism, which was diametrically opposed to the French. *Easter Morning* (Cat. 794), a relatively late work, reveals an already purified style reduced to the essential. The painting of Friedrich is deeply innovative; its only precedent is maybe found in the Dutch luminism of the 17th century. But the German artist breaks the interdependence of space and light in order to give privileged status to the light, taken as the symbol of the unity of nature. The direct influence of Friedrich did not extend further than the circle of his friends and pupils. However, as the historian Robert Rosenblum

166. Francisco José de Goya y Lucientes
Asensio Julia, c. 1798.

Oil on canvas. 54.5 x 41 cm.

792. Kaspar David Friedrich
Easter Morning, 1833.

Oil on canvas. 43.7 x 34.4 cm.

19th-Century European Painting from Romanticism to Realism

has recently demonstrated, his work is situated at the origin of an artistic tradition centered on the notion of the sublime, which is specifically Northern and modern and which traverses the 19th century and enters the 20th to reach as far as artists such as Rothko (see Room 46).

The unitary concept of nature as an organism in which the whole is greater than the sum of the parts constitutes a key notion in Romanticism. At the beginning of the 19th century it could be found in both Germany and England. Its most influential English expression, the philosophical poem of *The Prelude* by Wordsworth was a permanent source of inspiration for John Constable (1776-1837). *The Weir* (Cat. A 804) is a hymn to the English countryside which forms the background to the thoughts of Wordsworth or the walks of Jane Austen's characters. The influence of 17th-century Dutch landscape painting, and especially that of Jacob van Ruisdael, is patent, but this does not diminish the originality of Constable's style.

The two most important facets of French Realism are represented in the Museum. Gustave Courbet (1819-1877) raised the flag of political Realism. Creator of a deeply original style, he was also one of the best painters of the century. *The Stream, La Brème* (Cat. 495), painted when he had lost almost all of his artistic and political battles, is a demonstration of his talents as a born painter. Camille Corot (1796-1875) is difficult to classify. Romantic, Classicist and Realist, he was considered a master by the Impressionists. In *Setting Out for a Walk in the Parc des Lions at Port-Marly* (Cat. 494), painted in the last years of his life, the static figures of the distant children among the trees are illuminated with the silvery light of the Ile-de-France which so obsessed Pissarro and his friends.

A 804. **John R.A. Constable**
The Lock, 1824.

Oil on canvas. 142.2 x 120.7 cm.

The origin of Impressionism lies in the *Salon des Refusés* held in 1863 to show the work of the artists who had been refused by the official *Salon*, its members maintaining a systematic opposition to academic art from that point onwards. Contemporary critics and many subsequent historians saw in this movement the end of one historic cycle, that of classical painting, and the beginning of another, that of modern art. However, it must be stated that many of the ideas and a great deal of the stylistic formulae of Impressionism stem from 19th-century realism. Precedents can also be found in Constable and Turner and other more distant sources such as the 17th-century Dutch landscape and Venetian painting.

What then did the Impressionist revolution consist of? At the time there was talk of its rejection of historical, mythological and religious painting. What is significant here is the rejection of the contrast between two types of artistic expression: the 'formal', reserved for subjects of public importance, and the 'informal', suitable for other themes. The hierarchy implicit in this distinction was an essential part of the classical system and remained valid in academic and official circles in the second half of the 19th century. The landscape and everyday life in the city, the Impressionist themes *par excellence*, represent a preference for the 'commonplace' as opposed to the 'weightiness' of official art, and this is a first sign of modernity.

The second aspect of the Impressionist revolution concerns pictorial language. The Impressionists rejected the rules of academicism in favour of the freshness of individual expression and replaced the requirements of composition and form (perhaps the key concepts of classical painting) with the requirement that the painter should follow the impressions of colour registered on his retina. Light therefore became the central theme of painting to such an extent that some Impressionist painters, such as Monet in his famous series depicting Rouen Cathedral, painted different versions of the same subject at different times of day.

The Impressionists formed a coherent organised group from 1874, the date of their first group exhibition, until the first years of the following decade. As the artists in the group began to receive greater individual public acclaim the group began to break up.

The Museum contains works by the main Impressionist painters. We should first mention Edouard Manet (1832-1883).

659. Edouard Manet
Woman in Riding Habit, Fullface, c. 1882.

Oil on canvas. 73 x 52 cm.

712. Camille Pissarro
Saint-Honoré Street in the Afternoon. Effect of Rain, 1897.

Oil on canvas. 81 x 65 cm.

724. Pierre-Auguste Renoir
Woman with a Parasol in a Garden, c. 1873.

Oil on canvas. 54.5 x 65 cm.

Impressionist and Post-Impressionist Painting

Older than most of the other Impressionists, Manet never became firmly associated with the group. He more than anyone is responsible for the new emphasis on subjects taken from daily life and the value of the ephemeral. However, he was never convinced of the need to invent a systematic new language. In fact his style was based very much on a selected number of Old Masters dominated by Velázquez, Hals and especially Goya. In the *Woman in a Riding Habit, Full Face* (Cat. 659) produced in 1882, a year before his death, the treatment of light may be considered Impressionist. However, the marked contrast between the background and the figure and the freeness of the brushwork are reminiscent of Hals and distinguish Manet's style from that of the other Impressionists (although it must be remembered that this painting is unfinished).

The attitude of Edgar Degas (1834-1917) was sometimes close to that of Manet. He is separated from the rest of the Impressionist group by the importance he attributed to draughtsmanship and his acceptance of the authority of classical painting. Furthermore, no other Impressionist understood as well as he the character of the modern city and the decisive influence its way of life would have on artistic sensibility at the turn of the century. With the detached fascination of the *voyeur* he frequently used photographs to analyse the transformations the human body underwent in the work of seamstresses, laundresses, dancers, sportsmen, etc. In 1876-77 he began a series on ballet. *Dancer Swaying* (Cat. 515), which belongs to this series, uses the peculiar characteristics of the stage to experiment with pictorial space: while the dancers waiting in the wings are seen in frontal view, the performers seem to be on a different plane which the spectator observes from above as if in a box. Degas reinforces this distortion of space with his framing of the scene like a snapshot (or a Japanese print), cutting off the group of performers so that we only have a full view of the last in the line. We see part of the legs of the next one and the third is no more than a swirl of gauze. The real theme of the picture is constituted by these swirls, dotted with the sparkle of the sequins and fleetingly interrupted by by the white of the legs, emerging from a greenish background in which, as in the painting of Watteau and Titian, bodies and shadows blend into one another.

The three works by Degas in the Museum, including the one

515. Edgar Degas
Swaying Dancer (Dancer in Green), 1877-1879.

Pastel on paper. 66 x 36 cm.

reviewed above, are pastels. This technique, developed at the end of the 18th century, ensures greater purity of colour than any other, but requires a high level of skill in the execution in order to avoid commonplace results. Degas' mastery of pastel is revealed both in the precision of line in *Racehorses* (Cat. A 838) and the capacity for evoking the bright colours and textures of the feathers and materials that fill *At the Milliner's* (Cat. 516). For its technical virtuosity and its spatial complexity this last pastel can be considered one of Degas' masterpieces.

Claude Monet (1840-1926) contrasts with Degas in his systematic rejection of pictorial tradition. His style gradually abandons draughtsmanship, composition, perspective and volume to concentrate exclusively on the gradations of light and the qualities of colour. Both *The Cabin in Trouville* (Cat. A 856) and *The Thaw at Vétheuil* (Cat. 680) were done when Monet's language had reached maturity. The latter work belongs to a series of views of the Seine begun in 1878. Applying broken brushstrokes of contrasting colours the painter manages to reproduce with extraordinary precision the way the winter light falls on the snow and the flowing water.

Pierre Auguste Renoir (1841-1920) must be situated close to Monet. The pastel *Girl Seated in an Interior* (Cat. A 864) represents one of his most frequent themes, the depiction of women. *Wheat Field* (Cat. A 865) and *Woman with a Parasol* (Cat. 724) are landscapes. The latter was produced in 1873, at a time when Renoir was working frequently with Monet, and is a good example of the technical questions that occupied the attention of both artists at the time. The broken brushstrokes of vivid colours convert the surface of the canvas into a continuous tissue of dots and lines. It is the optical vibrancy of this surface recreates the impression of the flowery garden under the sun.

The landscape was the Impressionists' favourite genre. Practising it was what most united them with the general context of 19th-century painting. It was also what allowed painters who made concessions to tradition, such as Eugene Boudin (1824-1898) (Cat. 476, A. 833 and A. 834) and Armand Guillaumin (1841-1927) (Cat. A. 845), to later be considered Impressionists. Amongst the leading Impressionists, Alfred Sisley (1839-1899) and Camille Pissarro (1830-1903) painted practically nothing but landscapes. With little interest in theory,

680. Claude Monet
The Thaw at Vétheuil, 1881.

Oil on canvas. 60 x 100 cm.

516. **Edgar Degas**
At the Milliner's, c. 1883.

Pastel on paper. 75.9 x 84.8 cm.

Impressionist and
Post-Impressionist Painting

Sisley possessed a truly remarkable feeling for colour and a talent for brushwork. These are the qualities that make *The Flood in Port-Marly* (Cat. A 869) one of the most beautiful works in these rooms. Pissarro, who is usually considered the purest painter amongst the Impressionists, also displayed a similar lukewarm attitude to theory combined with confidence in his art. The Museum exhibits three of his works: two of them (Cat. 711 and A 861) are wooded landscapes done in the early 1870s at the beginnings of Impressionism. The third (Cat. 712) belongs to a celebrated series of views of Paris that the artist painted in the last years of the century. The freshness of the light soaked with drizzle falling on the street is typically Impressionist; in contrast, the geometric organisation of the composition reveals Pissarro's affinity with the young Neo-Impressionists in the last years of the century.

557. **Vincent van Gogh**
The Stevedores in Arles, 1888.

Oil on canvas. 54 x 65 cm.

The last exhibition of the Impressionists as a group took place in 1886. When Impressionism began to break up no other movement defined by a definite programme managed to achieve a comparable hegemony. Historians apply the label of Post-Impressionism to the art produced between that date and the first years of the twentieth century in Paris. The most outstanding tendencies of this period, Symbolism and Neo-Impressionism, lacked organisation and precise limits—the most important contributions to painting at the end of the century were made by isolated figures.

Despite his affinity with Symbolism, Paul Gaugin (1848-1903) can be considered an independent artist. The pictorial language of *Figure on a Road* (Cat. 552), painted in 1885, is still Impressionist and close to that of Pissarro. In the latter half of the 1880s, Gaugin became associated with a group of Symbolists. Painting for him was

559. **Vincent van Gogh**
"Les Vessenots" in Auvers, 1890.

Oil on canvas. 55 x 65 cm.

Impressionist and
Post-Impressionist Painting

no longer the registration of optical sensations but the expression of a spiritual world expressed in the work through the artist's emotions and moods, like music. In 1891 Gaugin left Europe to live in Polynesia. *Mata Mua* (Cat. A 842) forms part of a set of three works which the artist indicated in a letter of 1892 as being the culmination of everything he had produced until then. The title, which can be translated as 'Once upon a time' and the scene depicted, which refers to the cult of the Polynesian goddess of fertility, Hina, evoke a primitive world not yet polluted by modern man in which the fusion of man and nature attains the value of a religious experience. Both in this evocation of the primitive and for his pictorial language, based on bright, arbitrary colours and the absence of depth, Gaugin was one of the most influential artists for the following generation.

While Gaugin's primitivism is a symptom of the tragic conscience of modernity forged in the artistic and cultural circles of Europe towards the end of the century, the destiny of Vincent van Gogh (1853-1890) can be seen as its living incarnation. The Museum possesses three paintings representing three different moments of his short life as a painter. The oldest (Cat. 788) painted in 1885 belongs to the period in which Van Gogh was working in Nuenen in the Netherlands. It may be connected with the words he wrote in a letter to his brother Theo in the same year: 'one of the most beautiful things in this century has been to paint darkness, which at the same time is colour'. This still Post-Romantic twilight landscape contains the seed of the drama which bursts forth in the fiery sunset of *Stevedores in Arles* (Cat. 557), painted three years later, at the start of his fertile period in Provence. *Les Vessenots* (Cat. 559) displays the tortured brushwork characteristic of the landscapes he painted in Auvers-sur-Oise during the last months of his life.

Like Van Gogh, Henri de Toulouse-Lautrec (1864-1901) is an artist who cannot be classified as part of any group or tendency, but his Baudelairian talent situates him at the opposite extreme. His ironic, stylised vision of the modern city exercised a great influence on young artists at the turn of the century. The Museum possesses a group of lithographs on his most well-known subjects, which are exhibited on the balcony overlooking the central courtyard. It also has the two oils exhibited here, one of his friend *Gaston Bonnefoy* (Cat. 773) and the other of a regular model (Cat.

A 842. **Paul Gauguin**
Mata Mua (In Olden Times), 1892.

Oil on canvas. 91 x 69 cm.

774). In this very beautiful painting done in 1889, when Impressionism was disappearing as a movement, the painter was still making attempts to capture the effects of light. However, the thick brushwork and the construction of volume by facets evoke the Cézannian search for a style which would reunite the modernity of Impressionism with the solidity of the art in museums.

It was this synthesis which was to make Paul Cézanne (1839-1906) the most influential of 19th century artists in the 20th century. During the first half of his career as a painter Cézanne's style was close to that of the Impressionists, especially that of Pissarro, but his outstanding place in the history of painting is due to the work he produced between 1890 and 1906, the year of his death. *Portrait of a Farmer* (Cat. 488) constitutes a magnificent example of the pictorial style of those years. The light bathing the figure has the freshness and immediacy of the best Impressionist painting, but Cézanne uses colour to construct rather than to dissolve the volumes. It is this that makes the last work of Cézanne the departure point for the Cubism of Braque and Picasso. If the Impressionists looked to the facet of the Venetian heritage developed by Watteau and Turner, Cézanne seems to return to the central lesson of Titian and the High Renaissance. In doing so he opened the gates of the new century.

488. **Paul Cezanne**
Portrait of a Farmer, 1901-1906.

Oil on canvas. 65 x 54 cm.

34 Fauve Painting

At the turn of the century there arose a number of artistic movements which almost exclusively occupied the innovatory frontier of art until the arrival of Cubism. Fauvism in France and Expressionism in Germany were the most important examples.

These movements had the following characteristics in common: 1) The influence of the Post-Impressionist painters, especially Gaugin and Van Gogh. 2) The use of colour for symbolic and emotional purposes. 3) An expressionistic concept of artistic creation as the externalisation of the artist's emotional energy. 4) An attitude of rebellion towards bourgeois society, which in many cases led towards an overt sympathy for Anarchism.

Fauvism was born in 1905 from the decision of a group of young French artists to display their works together in the Salon d'Automne. The art critic Louis Vauxcelles described them as *fauves* (wild beasts) in irony, but the name soon stuck because it seemed a good characterisation of their pictorial style. The Fauves did not form an organised group and the movement was short-lived, beginning to break up in 1907.

Its key figure was Henri Matisse (1869-1954). *The Yellow Flowers* (Cat. 664) displayed in Room 36 was painted in 1902 before the Fauve group was constituted. Both the pictorial space and the use of colour seem to evoke the pastel works of Degas. Along with Matisse, André Derain (1880-1954) and Maurice Vlaminck (1876-1958) formed what the historian John Elderfield called 'the essential triangle of Fauvism'. Derain's *Waterloo Bridge* (Cat. 524) is one of the most brilliant examples of the Fauve style at its height. The influence of Van Gogh and the Neo-Impressionists is evident; but his work radiates an impersonal, purely physical energy which ascribes it to the sensibility of the new century. *Olive-Trees* (Cat. A 883) by Vlaminck, with its acid colouring and tormented brushwork, displays a high degree of dependence on Van Gogh.

From the so-called Le Havre group formed by the youngest Fauve painters the Museum presents only a work by Raoul Dufy (1877-1953). *Little Palm Tree* (Cat. A 839) belongs to a short but interesting series of oils dated around 1905 in which the artist attempts to evoke through almost flat colours the space and light of an interior with plants.

524. André Dera n
Waterloo Bridge, 1906.

Oil on canvas. 80.5 x 10" cm.

A 883. **Maurice Vlaminck**
Olive-Trees, 1905-1906.

Oil on canvas. 53.5 x 65 cm.

35-40 Expressionist Painting

Expressionism was a broad movement, a collective state of mind which lasted, with numerous changes and oscillations, from the end of the 19th until the middle of the 20th century.

It rested on a basic supposition: the work of art, rather than depicting the reality of the external world, must express a feeling or emotion. In contrast with Impressionism, which remained linked to the sensations and exterior vision of the world, Expressionism gave pride of place to the interior vision of the artist. From the stylistic point of view it represented the primacy of colour over draughtsmanship and an exaggerated distortion of form.

The works exhibited in rooms 36 to 40 illustrate the production of the main centres of Expressionism in Germany—Dresden, Berlin and Munich. The work of non-German artists related to Expressionism are shown in room 35.

The Norwegian painter Edvard Munch (1863-1944) exercised an important influence on the artists of Dresden and Berlin. *Evening (Evening Hour with the Artist's Sister)* (Cat. 689), a work of his youth, is impregnated with the the poetics of *fin-de-siècle* Symbolism. The feeling of isolation and depression which hangs over the female figure seated in the foreground seems to find its echo in the light and in the colour of the landscape. *Theatre of Masks* (Cat. 534) by the Belgian painter James Ensor (1860-1949), a contemporary of Munch, has a harsh, luminous colouring and an irregular draughtsmanship which distorts the forms, making them more unreal and at the same time more expressive.

Expressionism took root in *fin-de-siècle* Vienna, especially among artists from the younger generation such as Egon Schiele (1890-1918) and Oskar Kokoschka (1886-1980). Although the work of Gustav Klimt formed their point of departure, they moved away from the fluid and decorative line of his style. The network of horizontal and vertical lines that structures *Houses on the River. The Old Town* (Cat. 739) has a double function: a plastic one, to accentuate the flatness of the pictorial space, and an expressive one, to reinforce the impression of decadence that the artist associates with this urban landscape. Two genres stand out in Kokoschka's broad artistic production: landscape and the portrait. In the *Portrait of Max Schmidt* (Cat. 629) the rapid brushstroke and the contortion of the hands and gesture derive from Van Gogh, but the paroxysm to which Kokoschka carries these means of expression is characteristic of the works of his youth.

739. Egon Schiele
Houses on the River (The Old Town), 1914.

Oil on canvas. 100 x 120.5 cm.

689. Edvard Munch
Evening, 1888.

Oil on canvas. 75 x 100.5 cm.

Expressionist Painting

The first movement in German Expressionism to follow a definite programme was the *Die Brücke* (The Bridge) group, formed in Dresden in 1905, the same year as Fauvism appeared in Paris. It was formed at first by four young students of architecture: Ludwig Kirchner, Erich Heckel, Karl Schmidt-Rottluff and Fritz Bleyl. One of the most outstanding characteristics of the group was its cohesion and homogeneity. Searching for a common pictorial language, its members worked together and shared the same studios, models and clients.

The closest collaboration was that between Karl Schmidt-Rottluff (1884-1976) and Erich Heckel (1883-1970). The two artists spent long summer periods working in Dangast, Oldenburg, near the North Sea until 1912. Examples of this are *Autumn Landscape in Oldenburg* (Cat. 742) by Schmidt-Rottluff and *Brickworks. Dangast* (Cat. 579) by Heckel. The palette of bright greens, reds, yellows and blues seen in these paintings owes a great deal to Van Gogh.

Ernst Ludwig Kirchner (1880–1938) was undoubtedly the most important artist in the group. *Doris with Ruffled High Collar* (Cat. 613), *Clay Mine* (Cat. A. 853) and *Woman in a Birch Grove* (Cat. A. 854b) display the pictorial language that the members of *Die Brücke* shared in the initial years of he group. *Fränzi in front of Carved Chair* (Cat. 789) reflects the interest of the painter for primitive art. The model Fränzi, whose face appears in the foreground, was a girl of 11 who regularly posed for Kirchner and other members of the group. The little girl is seated in a chair carved by Kirchner himself, the back of which imitates an African mask; the contrast between the green tones of Fränzi's face and the pinks of the mask are noteworthy.

Although not a founder member of the group, Max Pechstein (1881-1955) joined *Die Brücke* in 1906. The Collection presents two works of his. *The Horse Market* (Cat. A. 860) was painted during the summer of 1910 in Moritzburg, near Dresden, and reveals certain influences from the Fauve painting with which Pechstein had come into contact in Paris in 1908. *Summer in Nidden* (Cat. 699) belongs to his mature period and reflects the primitivist orientation which was accentuated in his work after his voyage in 1914 to the Palau Islands in Oceania.

In 1911 the members of *Die Brücke* moved to Berlin. Their palette now became more simplified and the pictorial space distorted, moving away from the rules of perspective. Two of

742. Karl Schmidt-Rottluff
Autumn Landscape in Oldenburg, 1907.

Oil on canvas. 76 x 97.5 cm.

579. Erich Heckel
Brickworks, 1907.

Oil on canvas. 58 x 86 cm.

Expressionist
Painting

Kirchner's works displayed here belong to this period: *Curving Bay* (Cat. 618), an important landscape from the prewar years and *Berlin Street Scene with Streetwalker* (Cat. 614), which forms part of a series of Berlin cityscapes produced between 1913 and 1914. From 1917 onwards Kirchner lived in Switzerland, where he developed an even more violent artistic language, as can be seen in *Alpine Kitchen* (Cat. 616). The distortion of the space produces an impression of agitated movement and only the Alpine view in the background of the composition provides the scene with a point of restfulness.

Emil Nolde (1867-1956) joined *Die Brücke* in 1906 at the invitation of Schmidt-Rottluff, but left the group in the same year in order to follow his own path. *Summer Clouds* (Cat. 691) depicts a rough sea in which clouds and waves are treated as solid masses in motion. Nolde's style is based on the expressive use of colour, as

A 860. **Max Pechstein**
Horse Fair, 1910.

Oil on canvas. 70 x 81 cm.

789. **Ernst Ludwig Kirchner**
Fränzi in front of Carved Chair, 1910.

Oil on canvas. 71 x 49.5 cm.

can be appreciated in *Autumn Evening* (Cat. 690) of 1924 and *Sunflowers* (Cat. 692) of 1936.

In 1913, *Die Brücke* began to break up. A year earlier the *Der Blaue Reiter* (The Blue Rider) almanac edited by Kandinsky and Marc had appeared in Munich. A group of artists from different countries (Kandinsky, Marc, Macke, Jawlensky, Feininger, Itten, V. Burliuk, Klee, etc.) in frequent contact with the avant-garde of Paris congregated around this review. Influenced by the tradition of 19th-century German idealism, the artists in the group, especially Kandinsky, considered the mission of modern art one of liberating itself from its dependence on the external world in order to express the world of the spirit in a manner similar to that of music.

Of Russian origin, Wassily Kandinsky (1866-1944) lived in Munich from 1896 until his return to Russia in 1914. His discovery of abstract painting in 1910 was to make him one of the century's

691. **Emil Nolde**
Summer Clouds, 1913.

Oil on canvas. 73.3 x 88.5 cm.

616. **Ernst Ludwig Kirchner**
Alpine Kitchen, 1918.

Oil on canvas. 121.5 x 121.5 cm.

most important artists. Kandinsky's abstract paintings are displayed in Room 45. The two presented here, *Johannisstrasse in Murnau* (Cat. 611) and the *Ludwigskirche in Munich* (Cat. A. 852) are earlier works. They belong to a period when the painter was experimenting in an attempt to harmonise Post-Impressionism, Fauvism and Expressionism.

Franz Marc (1880-1916) is the other great figure in the *Blaue Reiter*. *The Dream* (Cat. 660) is an example of the group's exploration

of the spiritual. Marc created his own pictorial world in which animals appeared as symbols of beauty, purity and truth. He also developed a complicated artistic theory which attributed symbolic values to colours: blue represented the principle of masculinity, austere and spiritual, as opposed to yellow, the feminine principle, joyful and sensual, and red, the symbol of brutal, heavy matter. The mixing of these colours would produce the interpenetration of their respective values.

The youthful works of the Russian painter Alexej von Jawlensky (1864-1941), who went to live in Paris in 1905, reflect the influence of Matisse, with whom he worked for a time. In 1909 Jawlensky joined the *Blaue Reiter* in Munich. His paintings, *Child with Doll* (Cat. A. 850) and *The Red Veil* (Cat. 603) reveal not only Fauvist influence but also that of Russian icons in the frontality and calm of the personages portrayed.

August Macke (1887-1914), less interested than Kandinsky and Marc in theory, was perhaps the artist with the most Parisian influence of all the Munich group. *Circus* (Cat. 656) was produced shortly after his visit to Paris in 1912, where he met Delaunay. Lyonel Feininger (1871-1956) is another of the painters from the *Blaue Reiter* group influenced by Delaunay. The Museum possesses various works of his. *The White Man* (Cat. A 840) is reminiscent of his stage as a caricaturist in Paris. In *Architecture II (The Man from Potin)* (Cat. 545) and *The Lady in Mauve* (Cat. 543) the juxtaposition of planes contains affinities with Cubism. Johannes Itten (1888-1967) was an independent Swiss Expressionist who collaborated with the Bauhaus in the 1920s. *Group of Houses in Spring. Stuttgart by the Killesberg* (Cat. 602) structured by a series of circles, triangles and geometrical forms is an example of the application of the principles of musical composition to painting.

Max Beckmann (1881-1950) occupies a singular place in the history of 20th-century art. In 1912 he abandoned Expressionism to embark upon a career as a realist inspired by the great German tradition of late Gothic and Grünewald. He later coincided with the *New Objectivity* in its critique of German society. From then onwards his most important works were allegorical compositions with great pictorial and expressive force. The Museum contains four works which provide an excellent illustration of his evolution. His *Self-Portrait with Raised Hand* (Cat. 465) of 1908 is still close to *fin-de-siècle* painting such as that of Corinth and Lieberman. *Quappi*

660. **Franz Marc**
The Dream, 1912.

Oil on canvas. 100.5 x 135.5 cm.

A 852. **Wassily Kandinsky**
The Ludwigskirche in Munich, 1908.

Oil on board. 67.3 x 96 cm.

in Pink (Cat. 464) is a portrait of his second wife, Quappi (Mathilde von Kaulbach), whom the artist painted frequently. Here, she is presented frontally, imbued with the calm force of her own personality. *Still Life with Yellow Roses* (Cat. 463) is an example of the painter's interest in the problems of colour. *Artists* (Cat. A. 831), an allegorical composition related to the triptychs of the 1940s, was painted in the United States two years before his death.

The last phase of German Expressionism is known as *New Objectivity (Neue Sachlichkeit)*. This movement responded to the climate of crisis in post-war Berlin, the scene of the economic, political and moral collapse of Bismarck's Germany. Urban themes allowed artists to express their political attitude or criticisms of society. An objective style with great precision and clarity was born as a reaction against the subjectivism of Expressionism. *New Objetivity* coincided chronologically with a return to figurative art in the rest of Europe in the 1920s (see room 45); like this movement, it involved a revaluation of Renaissance painting, in this case that of Germany.

The portrait was a very common genre among the *New Objectivity* painters. In Room 40 there are other good examples. By Christian Schad (1894-1982), one of the painters with the greatest obsession for detail in the group, are the *Portrait of Dr. Haustein* (Cat. 733) of 1928 and *Maria and Annunziata from the Harbour* (Cat. 734) of 1923. Those of Rudolf Schlichter (1890-1955), *Oriental Journalist* (Cat. 741), and Albert Henrich (1899-1971), *Portrait of the Painter A. M. Tränkler,* are closer to the expressive naturalism of the pre-war period. *Twice Hilde II* (Cat. 596) by Karl Hubbuch (1891-1980) is the left half of a square canvas depicting four different aspects of the model. The canvas was divided by Hubbuch himself in the 1950s.

The two most important artists in the movement were Otto Dix (1891-1969) and George Grosz (1893-1959). Grosz was a very politically active painter and a great draughtsman. The Museum contains one of his most emblematic works, *Metropolis* (Cat. 569) from 1916-1917, representing an urban scene with a crowd running in different directions. In this work constructed like a giant collage, Cubist and Futurist influences are clearly visible. But in contrast with the Futurist glorification of the city, Grosz's vision has a markedly apocalyptic character.

At the beginning of the 1920s, Grosz and the artists of the Berlin avant-garde hardened their political stance. This led many of them

464. Max Beckmann
Quappi in pink jumper, 1932-1935.

Oil on canvas. 105 x 73 cm.

to adopt a satirical realism which could be understood by everybody. The Museum possesses important works on paper along with an oil, *Street Scene (Kurfürstendamm)* (Cat. 572), which illustrate this aspect of Grosz's painting.

Dix attained his artistic maturity with a series of precise portraits, one of the best examples of which is that of *Hugo Erfurth with a Dog* (Cat. 525). Dix's style takes inspiration from the German masters of the Renaissance, not only in form but also in the technique of tempera on panel.

The coming to power in Germany of the Nazis in 1933 meant the end of *New Objectivity* and all manifestations of modern art, which were to be officially described as 'degenerate art'. Many of the most representative works of German Expressionism were destroyed and the artists obliged to cease practising or go into exile.

525. **Otto Dix**
Hugo Erfurth With a Dog, 1926.

Tempera and oil on plywood panel. 80 x 100 cm.

569. **George Grosz**
Metropolis (View of the Metropolis), 1916-1617.

Oil on canvas. 100 x 102 cm.

GROUND FLOOR

41-44 The Experimental Avant-gardes

The changes which took place in the visual arts at the beginning of the 20th century were probably the greatest in their history. Although the term 'avant-garde' is sometimes used to designate the innovations of modern art generically, it is recommendable to reserve it for those which occurred between approximately 1907 (the beginning of the search which was to lead to Cubism) and 1924 (the publication of the First Surrealist Manifesto). The main characteristics of the innovations during this period were: 1) The desire to break with existing art, each movement applying this especially to its most immediate precursors. 2) The conviction that art, like language, depends on a set of conventional rules and that the most profound artistic innovations consist of replacing one set of rules with another. 3) Faith in the progress of history. 4) As a consequence of all the above, the predisposition to consider the work of art as: a) an example of a new set of rules proposed in polemical fashion; b) an action announcing the future; c) an experiment like those which mark scientific progress.

Avant-gardism thus defined was a dominant attitude in modern art during the period of its affirmation in relation to the art of the past. Once a modern sensibility had been assumed the work of art ceased to be conditioned by the rules of doctrine and more importance was ascribed to its singularity as an individual work. Some artists, such as Picasso, abandoned the avant-garde relatively early, around 1913 or 1914, others at a later date. In general terms it can be stated that avant-gardism began to separate from the central current of modern art in the late 1920s, to become totally marginalised after the Second World War. It was reborn at the end of the 1960s, now deprived of polemical bite, and spread in academic and institutional circles.

The most important avant-garde movements from the period before the First World War were Cubism and Futurism.

Cubism was born from the collaboration of Pablo Ruiz Picasso (1881-1973) and Georges Braque (1882-1963) between 1908 and 1914. Initially limited to the work of these two painters, it began to spread amongst artists working in Paris in 1910. If the Impressionists, Post-Impressionists and Fauves captured the fleeting moment, impressions and moods, placing importance on light and colour in the painting, Braque and Picasso, taking Cézanne as their point of departure, centered their attention on volume and space. *Still Life. Glasses and Fruit* (Cat. 708) and *The Park of Carrières Saint-Denis*

710. **Pablo Ruiz Picasso**
Man with a Clarinette, 1911-1912.

Oil on canvas. 106 x 69 cm.

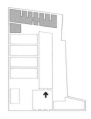

(Cat. 479) belong to the initial phase. A comparison of these works with *Woman with a Mandolin* (Cat. 478) and *Man with a Clarinet* (Cat. 710) allows us to understand the evolutionary process that led Cubism to its culmination. The first step was a reduction of forms to geometrically simple volumes. Then came a sort of flattening of volumes on the pictorial plane, as if they were being viewed simultaneously from two points of view, and a rhythmic structuring of this plane. In order to reinforce the rhythmic effect the points of view were multiplied and the volumes became increasingly incomplete and open, leading to them appearing to dissolve into the surrounding space. Finally, schematic lines or signs distributed in a framework of tiny facets were all that was left of form. The vibration of the light in this framework evokes the depth of space.

When it reached this point, Cubism seemed to be heading towards completely abstract painting. Perhaps the most eloquent example of this transition is Piet Mondrian (1872-1944), as can be seen in *Grey/Blue Composition* (Cat. 678). However, Braque and Picasso chose a different path. For them abstract painting, condemned to express only states of mood, obeyed a nineteenth century sensibility. Seeking a new plastic form suited to the new century they made efforts to reintroduce physical corporeality into painting. The first step consisted of modifying the framework through a centripetal composition which allowed the presence of objects to be accentuated. They then introduced colour and texture. Finally they abandoned the framework to create a new space, constructed like a collage, through the juxtaposition of contrasting planes. *Man's Head* (Cat. 707) by Picasso illustrates the painting of this phase, known as Synthetic Cubism, which was in fact marks Picasso and Braque's transition from Cubism to a post-avant-garde position.

The Cubism of Juan Gris (1887-1927) followed its own course. During the second decade he maintained a lineal structure deriving from Analytical Cubism, but with colour playing a basic role, as can be seen in *The Smoker* (Cat. 567). *Seated Woman* (Cat. A. 843) is one of the best works of these years of plenitude; the relationships between light and colour, superimposed against an abstract geometrical framework, evoke the presence of the female figure. *Bottle and Fruit-Dish* (Cat. 566) announces the style of the 1920s.

The historian Douglas Cooper included Léger along with Gris, Braque and Picasso in what he called 'essential Cubism' in order to distinguish it from the work of other artists. However, the breaking

A 843. **Juan Gris**
Sitting woman, 1917.

Oil on panel. 116 x 73 cm.

down of forms in his paintings owes more to the study of movement in Delaunay and the Futurists than to Picasso and Braque's analysis of volumes. *The Staircase. (Second State)* (Cat. 645) belongs to the group called 'contrasts of forms' from the years 1913 and 1914, the culmination of Léger's Cubism.

Futurism was an Italian movement predominantly literary in scope founded in 1909 by Filippo Maria Marinetti. His doctrine can be resumed as the exaltation of conflict, speed and the future. The

634. **Frantisek Kupka**
Localization of Graphic Mobiles, 1912-1913.

Oil on canvas. 200 x 194 cm.

645. Fernand Léger
The Staircase (Second State), 1914.

Oil on canvas. 88 x 124.5 cm.

Manifesto of Futurist Painting was published in 1910. *Patriotic Demonstration* (Cat. 459) by Giacomo Balla (1871-1958), the most mature amongst the artists to sign the manifesto, illustrates one of the tendencies of pictorial Futurism. Balla renders the waving of the flags and the movements of the demonstrators as a rhythmic series of curved superimposed volumes in which echoes of *Art Nouveau* can be perceived. The other tendency can be illustrated with the work of Gino Severini (1883-1966), a painter who lived in Paris from 1896 and went through an evolution from Neo-Impressionism to Cubism parallel with that of the Duchamp brothers, Delaunay and Kupka. *Expansion of the Light* (Cat. 752), a luminous space painted using a pointillist technique, which dilates with rhythmical dancing movements illustrates the most advanced aspect of Futurism before the war.

Most of the innovations in painting during the second decade can be understood as combinations of: a) the Cubist method of breaking down forms; b) the Futurist method of depicting movement; c) the search for a new understanding of colour stemming from

The Experimental
Avant-gardes

Seurat. The possibilities these combinations opened up to painting can be appreciated in *Woman with a Parasol. The Parisian* (Cat. 517) by Robert Delaunay and in *Simultaneous Contrasts* (Cat. 518) by his wife Sonia Terk. The poet Guillaume Apollinaire gave birth to the term 'Orphic Cubism' for the paintings of the Delaunays. He included with them the Duchamp brothers and the Czech painter Frantisek Kupka (1871-1957).

Both the Delaunays and Kupka experimented with abstract painting in 1909-1910, at the same time as Kandinsky was doing so in Munich. This was no coincidence: it stemmed from the very widespread idea at the end of the 19th century that there are deep analogies between the different forms of artistic expression, particular between painting and music. *Study for the Language of Verticals* (Cat. 790) directly, almost naively, exploits this analogy. The integration of Kupka in the Orphic group enriched his painting, as can be seen in *Localisation of Graphic Movements I* (Cat. 634), a masterwork from his early period.

Mikhail Larionov (1881-1964) defined Rayonnism, the movement he founded in Moscow in 1913 with Natalia Gontcharova (1881-1962), as a synthesis of Cubism, Futurism and Orphism. *Street with Lanterns* (Cat. 636) was painted before this date, but announces the new style. The best example of its plenitude in the Museum is *Rayonnist Landscape. The Forest* (Cat. 562) by Natalia Gontcharova.

No one in the Russian avant-garde of the second decade assimilated Cubism better than the painter Liubov Popova (1889-1924). *Still Life (Instruments)* (Cat. 715) is a key work for understanding his evolution towards abstraction under the influence of Malevich. The two works entitled *Pictorial Architectonic* and *Architectonic Composition* (Cat. 714 and 716) belong to a series produced between 1916 and 1918 which was already completely abstract.

The Russian revolution opened a propitious period for avant-garde artists. The break with the past, the emphatic affirmation of the future and the spirit of experiment were attitudes which now predominated in all spheres of social life. The principal tendencies of the Russian revolutionary avant-garde were Suprematism and Constructivism. The leader of Suprematism was Kasimir Malevich. In addition to the *Pictorial Architectonics* of Popova mentioned above, other paintings of the Museum which can be ascribed to this

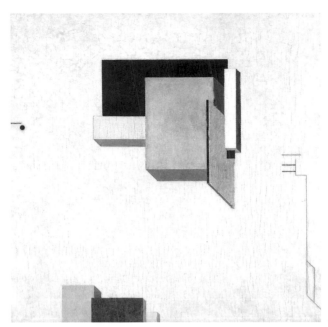

652. Eliezer Lissitzky
Proun 1 C, 1919.

Oil on plywood. 68 x 68 cm.

675. Laszló Moholy-Nagy
Large Railway Painting, 1920.

Oi¹ on canvas. 100 x 77 cm.

The Experimental
Avant-gardes

tendency are the *Composition* (Cat. 625) by Ivan Kliun (1843-1943) and the magnificent *Suprematist Composition* (Cat. 506) by Ilya Chasnik (1902-1929), a late work which has stylistic affinities with Constructivism.

The central idea of Constructivism, whose first leader was the sculptor Tatlin, but in whose development the contribution of architects such as the Vesnin brothers was decisive, is that the work of art must not represent anything, not even abstract images, but limit itself to expressing the rules which govern its construction in space. One of the consequences of this doctrine was the breaking down of the differences between architecture, sculpture and painting. The works that El Lissitzky (1890-1941) called 'Prouns' are a good example of the transition from Suprematism to Constructivism. In *Proun 1C* (Cat. 652), one of the artist's most beautiful works, the subtlety of the colour and the central disposition of the figures are reminiscent of Malevich. *Proun 4B* (Cat. 651) already reveals the spatial dynamism characteristic of Constructivism.

The relationships between the artistic and political vanguards cooled in the 1920s and ended at the beginning of the following decade with the disappearance of avant-garde art and the imposition of the so-called 'social realism' by the authorities of the Soviet state.

Between 1922 and 1925 Lissitzky worked in Germany and Switzerland. His stay contributed to the development of the Central European avant-garde. The most important artists with whom he was in contact were Lázló Moholy-Nagy (1895-1946), Kurt Schwitters (1887-1948) and Theo van Doesburg (1883-1931). *Large Railway Painting* (Cat. 675) is a key work from Moholy-Nagy's first period. After his contact with Lissitzky the artist was provided with the opportunity of developing his own version of Constructivism after joining the Bauhaus, a school of art, architecture and design created with the aim of integrating the different disciplines, in 1923. The name of Kurt Schwitters (1887-1948) is generally associated with Dadaism, a movement which arose during the war. Although very active, the Dada movement did not aspire to coherence and Schwitters was perhaps the most independent of its members. As of 1919 his activity was channeled towards the collage and *assemblage*. *Merzbild 1A* (Cat. 746) is one of the first *assemblages*. Although it contains reminiscences of Expressionism, the assembled elements function more than anything through their material

746. **Kurt Schwitters**
Merzbild 1A (The Psychiatrist), 1919.

Mixed media, montage on canvas. 48.5 x 38.5 cm.

The Experimental Avant-gardes

qualities. This is the basis on which Schwitters evolved during the 1920s, coming close to Constructivism, as can be seen in the magnificent *Picture To Be Seen from Eight Sides* (Cat. 745).

The *De Stijl* group founded in 1917, to which Theo van Doesburg (1883-1931) belonged, was the main exponent of experimental European avant-gardism during the inter-war period. It proposed a reduction of the language of the visual arts to its basic components: the primary colours and horizontals and verticals. *Composition* (Cat. 526) is an important example of the application of these rules from Van Doesburg and Mondrian's period of greatest mutual influence. The extreme rigour but also the enormous power of visual attraction of his work have made Piet Mondrian (1872-1944) one of the great myths of the century. In addition to the Cubist composition mentioned above, a transitional work, the Museum presents two other works by him: *Composition I* (Cat. 677) is a classical example of clarity, simplicity and monumentality from his mature period, and *New York City, New York* (Cat. 679), a marvellous hymn to modern life, started during the war, which remained unfinished due to his death.

It would perhaps be no exaggeration to attribute part of the submerged affinity which links the work of Mondrian with the central current of the history of painting to his association during 1916-1918 with Bart van der Leck (1876-1949), a painter from Utrecht who, after having been a founder member, left *De Stijl* at the early date of 1918. Few historians would place Van der Leck in the list of the principal artists of the century; but *Woodhacker* (Cat. 642) is one of the most beautiful paintings in the Museum.

679. Piet Mondrian
New York City, New York, c. 1942.

Oil, pencil, charcoal and painted tape on canvas. 117 x 110 cm.

45-46 The Synthesis of Modernity

In 1932 the historian Henry Russell Hitchcock and the architect Philip Johnson organised an exhibition of architecture in the Museum of Modern Art (MoMA) of New York on the initiative of its director, Alfred H. Barr. Although the works exhibited came from different avant-garde groups, the authors identified a common style in modern architecture which they called the 'International Style'. In the case of painting and sculpture, however, Barr did not seek to establish a common style. He organised two exhibitions which traced out, as if on a map, the main routes followed in the evolution of modern art: 1) From Cubism to Abstraction, and 2) Fantastic Art, Dada and Surrealism. The 1930s saw various initiatives which, like Barr's, sought a synthetic vision of modern art. These were the foundations of the developments which would take place after the Second World War: the creation of specialist magazines, the organisation of large group exhibitions, the opening of museums and entry into the universities and art schools, milestones in a process which would lead modern art to a position of hegemony, which would culminate around 1960.

These external indications of a process of convergence and synthesis are paralleled by internal ones, which were inherent to the consciousness of artistic creation. Some can already be found in the 1920s. A significant example is that of so-called 'Synthetic Cubism', a stylistic label which arose during the First World War. In contrast with Analytical Cubism, Synthetic Cubism did not imply a new set of rules. It was a form of painting which spread through imitation, analogy or metamorphosis. This absence of rules and the capacity to adapt to different currents of taste were precisely the qualities which allowed it to endure and become one of the most influential plastic languages in modern art.

Practically all the paintings Georges Braque (1882-1963) did after his return from the war in 1917 could be described as Synthetic Cubism. The pictorial space of *The Pink Tablecloth* (Cat. 480) continues to be Cubist in the same way as his collages of 1913 and 1914. At the same time the biomorphic forms, the monumental composition, the earthy textures and the dull palette point towards what would be an important current of taste in the 1940s.

Composition. 'The Disk' (Cat. 643) forms part of a group of works that Fernand Léger (1881-1955) painted upon his return from the war which evoke the mechanical turbulence of urban life. It could be described as an adaptation of the Orphic painting of the

709. **Pablo Ruiz Picasso**
Harlequin with a Mirror, 1923.

Oil on canvas. 100 x 81 cm.

The Synthesis
of Modernity

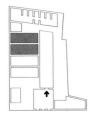

pre-war period to the new spatial geometry of Synthetic Cubism. In *The Bridge* (Cat. 855), painted five years later, we find the same spatial geometry, but the painting evokes a static luminous world. The difference is also due to a change of taste; Léger had joined the ranks of those who, in their search for a new order, abandoned Cézanne to follow Seurat, as André Salmon put it in 1920.

Picasso too, to a certain extent, figures in their number. The desire for peace and order is always associated with the Classicist figurativeness found in his work during these years. However, although they sometimes coincide, Classicism and return to order are not necessarily identical: *The Three Musicians* of 1921, in the MoMA, the most celebrated example of his Synthetic Cubism, reflects the return to order to no less an extent than *The Flute of Pan,* a Classicist painting of 1923. Moreover, although *Harlequin with a Mirror* (Cat. 709) is also a Classicist painting from the same year, its inspiration is totally different. Only the face reveals any resemblance to the bathers in *The Flute of Pan.* In reality it is a mask. Harlequin is at this time a representation of Picasso himself, an evocation of this soujourn in Italy and his meeting with Olga, who was now his wife. The figure looking at himself in the mirror is, as in Baroque painting, a metaphor for the passage of time. Stylistically the painting looks like an assemblage of pieces painted by different hands. The white cloths have an implausible corporeality and the impastos of colour give the trunk a disordered carnality. Everything gives off an air of bitter melancholy.

In the same year, André Breton had published an article in which he attacked Cubism but 'saluted in the work of Picasso the first expression in modern art of a quality of *illegality'.* This rejection of rules and codes would have a twofold effect on the development of Surrealism: it would guarantee its influence throughout the process of affirmation of modern art, and simultaneously maintain ambiguity as to its affiliation. Certain famous artists outside the movement could be claimed as belonging to it; others generally considered Surrealist, such as Ernst or Miró, could maintain themselves at a distance for long periods and evolve in their own ways.

It may be said of Max Ernst (1891-1976) that he interiorised the Surrealist plurality of languages. The Museum presents three of his works which are all totally different from each other. *Untitled* (Cat. 538) and *33 Girls Looking for a White Butterfly* (Cat. 537) are

672. Joan Miró
Catalan Peasant with a Guitar, 1924.

Oil on canvas. 148 x 114 cm.

The Synthesis of Modernity

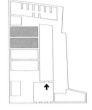

exhibited in Room 45. *Solitary and Conjugal Trees* (Cat. 535) is exhibited in Room 47.

Psychic automatism is a basic principal of Surrealism requiring the elimination of all rational control over creativity. In the field of poetry it took the form of writing based on the spontaneous associations of words. In that of painting, visual images would be associated spontaneously, as in dreams. There are two possible ways of doing this: representing images with a conventional technique, a 'photographic' technique, as with Dalí, or by means of an 'automatic' technique of painting, itself based on spontaneity. Joan Miró (1893-1983) was the main representative of this second manner. *Catalan Peasant with a Guitar* (Cat. 672) illustrates the artist most radical moment. *Composition* (Cat. A. 886) belongs to a group of imaginary landscapes of 1926 and 1927. *'L'Oiseau éclair aveuglé par le Feu de la Lune'* (Cat. 674) is a beautiful miniature whose pictorial language derives from the famous *Constellations* series.

In the MoMA exhibition mentioned above, Barr presented Dadaism and Surrealism as a continuation of a fantastic tradition with roots in the Middle Ages, and Klee, Kandinsky and Chagall as the continuers of this same tradition in the 20th century. Born in Russia, Marc Chagall (1887-1985) settled in Paris in 1910 and came into contact with Léger and the Orphist group. In *The House in Grey* (Cat. 500) a work painted shortly after his return to Russia in 1914, the influence of the Parisian avant-gardists is still visible. *The Rooster* (Cat. 499) and *Madonna of the Village* (Cat. 497) are characteristic examples of the style he developed after his definitive return to France in 1922, a form of painting based on the Jewish popular culture of the Russia of his childhood.

Wassily Kandinsky (1866-1944) and Paul Klee (1879-1940) participated in Munich in *Der Blaue Reiter* (see Room 38). From the departure point of the Expressionist landscape, Kandinsky's painting went through a number of transpositions to arrive in 1910-1911 at what he called abstract painting. The artist sought inpure colour, devoid of figurative references, that power of unleashing a torrent of images and feeling which is usually attributed to music. The effect can be seen in *Picture with Three Spots* (Cat. nº 609). Despite their biographical coincidences, Kandinsky and Klee represent two contrasting artistic temperaments. The musical analogy is important for both, but in very different ways, Klee sought in music not so much a torrent of sensations as what it contained of combinatory art or

609. Wassily Kandinsky
Picture with Three Spots, 1914.

Oil on canvas. 121 x 111 cm.

play. *Revolving House* (Cat. n° 624) is like a lesson in descriptive geometry finishing in ecstasy. *Omega 5* (Cat. n° 625) falls within the Gothic tradition of the grotesque, which for Klee plays a role similar to the one Mediterranean Classicism played for Picasso.

Neither Klee nor Kandinsky lived to see the end of the war. Among its consequences for the history of art we could mention two which might have surprised them: modern art was on the winning side and New York became the privileged scenario of artistic

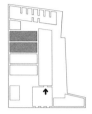

innovation. The most important of these new tendencies is the one known as Informalism in Europe and Abstract Expressionism in the United States. Two precedents are normally ascribed to this movement: the Cubist space and Surrealist automatism. The former was well known in the United States during the 1930s. Lesser acquaintance with the latter was compensated for by the emigration of a large part of the Surrealist group from Paris to New York in 1939 at the outbreak of the war. Arshile Gorki (1905-1948), a painer who had carefully studied Picasso during the 1930s, was one of the first American artists to adopt Surrealist automatism. In *Hugging* (Cat. 563) it is possible to discern a spatial structure derived from Cubist geometry onto which a colouring revealing the influence of Miró is superimposed. *Last Painting* (Cat. 564) reveals a third factor: the German Expressionist tradition. Its influence is better appreciated in Willem de Kooning (1904). In *Abstraction* (Cat. 630), an important early work, a furious wind of colour rends the scaffolding of the

563. **Arshile Gorky**
Hugging/ (Good Hope Road II) / (Pastoral), 1945.

Oil on canvas. 64.7 x 82.7 cm.

713. Jackson Pollock
Brown and Silver I, c. 1951.

Enamel and silver paint on canvas. 145 x 101 cm.

post-Cubist space. *Red Man with Moustache* (Cat. 631) has an almost identical palette to the one used by the *Die Brücke* artists in 1907. The Cubist space has disappeared, there remains only a non-figurative space, purely optic, which materialises in the free play of the brushstrokes on the canvas.

This new type of space is surely the most important invention of post-war painting. *Brown and Silver I* (Cat. 713) by Jackson Pollock (1912-1956) is a classical example of the method which led to its discovery: the taking of Surrealist automatism to its ultimate consequences, applying it to the very gesture with which the colour is applied to the canvas. But the same effect can be obtained by other methods. This is revealed by *Green on Maroon* (Cat. 729) by Mark Rothko (1903-1970) and *Earth Rhythms* (Cat. 771) by Mark Tobey (1890-1976). Although they are painted in very different manners, one with the superposition of broad transparent glazes, the other by the accumulation of a series of minuscule calligraphic patterns, the pulsing vibration of their pictorial space depends in both cases on colour.

The European artists, especially Lucio Fontana, also arrived at a similar pictorial space. If one would like to characterize this, one ought to remember the precedents suggested by Rosenblum (see Room 31): the absolute and luminous space in which the figures Malevich and Kliun (see Room 43) float, and in a last instance the space that cuts off Friedrich's horizons.

Fontana's work *The gold of Venice* (Cat. 547), which is located in the Central Courtyard, could maybe suggest older origins.

729. **Mark Rothko**
Green on Maroon, 1961.

Mixed media on canvas. 258 x 229 cm.

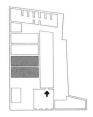

The process of synthesis described in the previous chapter concluded at the beginning of the 1960s with an historic turning point coinciding with the general acceptance of modern art. Although the following period is still very close at hand, it can safely be said that the dominant tendency which emerged was that of Pop Art. The Museum possesses a set of high-quality works representing this tendency. They are accompanied by other works representing minority pictorial languages or ones marginal to the central current of modern art.

The most important of these marginal languages is that of Surrealism. When we referred to this movement in the previous chapter we spoke about the representation of spontaneous associations of images, such as those from dreams, by means of a conventional pictorial language. The artist who best represents this concept of Surrealism is Salvador Dalí (1904-1989). In *Dream Caused by the Flight of a Bee around a Pomegranate a Second before Awakening* (Cat. 510) the wife of the artist, Gala, is depicted sleeping nude in the centre of a fantastic landscape full of dream images. In contrast with Dalí's painting, Ives Tanguy (1900-1955) depicts a desolate universe, with unidentifiable beings and objects. René Magritte (1898-1967) was a founding member of the Belgian Surrealist group. Although his painting technique was also conventional, Magritte was not interested in the subconscious; his associations of images revealed conceptual paradoxes. In *The Key to the Fields* (Cat. 657) the artist painted a window with a view of a country landscape. The glass is broken and the same landscape is seen as a painted image on the fallen fragments; we do not know if the window is transparent or opaque, real or fictitious.

Figurative painting, a minority manner of expressing modern sensibility, has been expressed over the course of the 20th century by different schools. One of the most outstanding in American painting was Precisionism, which developed in the 1930s and had certain features in common with New Objectivity in Germany. Charles Sheeler (1883-1965), the most famous of the Precisionists, is the painter of *Canyons* (Cat. 757), an impersonal representation of the skyscrapers and office blocks which could be found in the middle of any American city. *Highway over the Sea* (Cat. A 837) by Ralston Crawford (1906-1978) appears to anticipate certain currents in Pop Art by a quarter of a century.

Ben Shahn (1898–1969) is the most outstanding representative

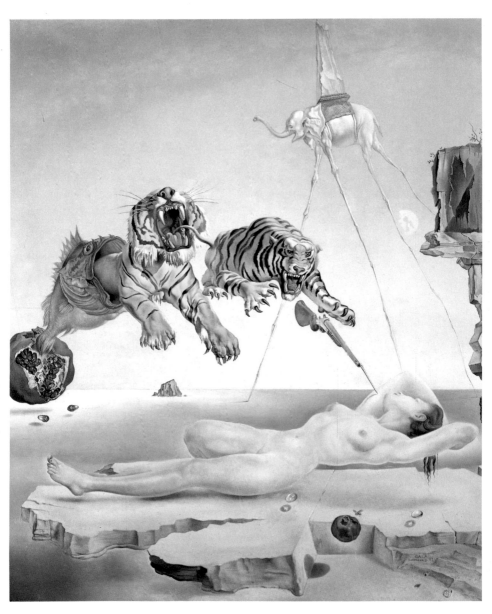

510. Salvador Dalí
*Dream caused by the Flight of a Bee Around a
Promegranate a Second before Awakening, 1944.*

Oil on panel. 51 x 41 cm.

of Social Realism, a movement which emerged after the crisis of 1929 in reply to the economic depression. Like other politically committed artists of his time, Shahn frequently worked as an illustrator and this left a permanent mark on his work. *Four Piece Orchestra* (Cat. 754) depicts three men enjoying a moment of leisure, two of them dressed as workers. In *Carnival* (Cat. 756) a man is sleeping in a public park far removed from the happiness of the passing couples.

Edward Hopper (1882-1967) is perhaps the most important realist painter of the 20th century. His painting incorporates stylistic features from the history of European painting from Piero della Francesca to Vermeer of Delft. *Girl at a Sewing Machine* (Cat. 595) belongs to a series depicting women working in domestic interiors. In *Hotel Room* (Cat. 594) the scene is dominated by the figure of the girl seated on the bed reading a train timetable, while the harsh electric light of the room makes the night seen through the window even darker.

Balthus (1908) is one of the most well-known European figurative artists. His painting is situated on the margins of modernity and attempts to capture the metaphysical atmosphere of Quattrocento art. *The Card Game* (Cat. 460) is a significant example of the search for monumentality and the implicit erotic atmosphere that characterises his style.

The London School, which included painters such as Michael Andrews (1928), Leon Kossoff (1926), Frank Auerbach (1931) and Lucien Freud (1922) is perhaps the most consistent group in post-Second World War figurative painting. Although they differed stylistically, these artists shared an interest in the human figure and urban landscapes. They also shared a certain air of Expressionism rarely made explicit. The best represented in the Museum is Freud, whose painting exploits the deformations resulting from unusual viewpoints. *Reflection with Two Children* (Cat. 550) from 1965 and *Large Interior. Paddington* (Cat. 549) from 1968-1969 are perfect illustrations of these characteristics. *Portrait of Baron H. H. Thyssen-Bornemisza* (Cat. 551) is set against the background of Watteau's *Pierrot Content*, which also belongs to the Collection (see Room 28).

Francis Bacon (1909-1992) was a painter close to the London School, although he is better known and older than them. His style, which can be related to the Surrealist and Expressionist traditions is

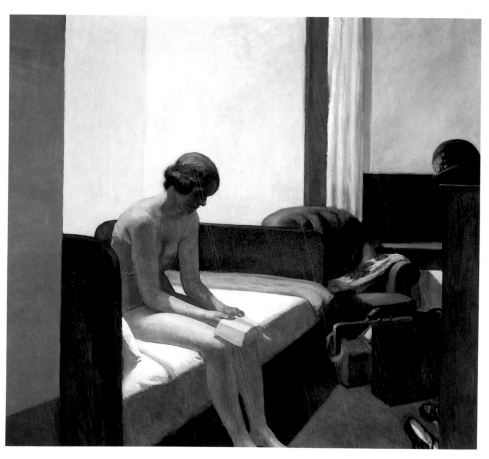

594. Edward Hopper
Hotel Room, 1931.

Oil or canvas. 152.4 x 165.7 cm.

far removed from traditional figurativeness. Bacon's paintings frequently reveal bare rooms with isolated figures which have been expressively distorted. *Portrait of George Dyer in a Mirror* (Cat. 458) is a portrait of a friend who was also his habitual model in the 1960s.

The last room in the Museum contains a group of works which can be ascribed to Pop Art. This term was first used by the critic Lawrence Alloway to designate an artistic movement which arose in England at the end of the 1950s. It was based on an awareness of technological modernisation and its cultural consequences, especially in the field of communication. The language of Pop Art is characterised by the presence of images extracted from advertising, comics and the mass media. However, the change of direction brought about by Pop Art went beyond iconography, being equivalent to a profound reconsideration of the modern project comparable with that of early Baroque in relation to the art of the Renaissance and Mannerism (see Room 12). Thus, in contrast with the features which characterised modern art in its mature period,

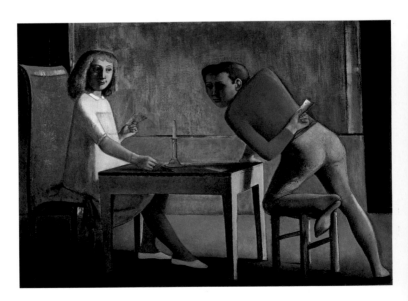

460. **Balthus**
The Card Game, 1948-1950.

Oil on canvas. 140 x 194 cm.

458. Francis Bacon
Portrait of George Dyer in a Mirror, 1968.

Oil on canvas. 198 x 147 cm.

Surrealism, Figurative
Tradition and Pop Art

Pop art: 1) Is extrovert and aspires to make the work of art objective or impersonal. 2) Gives symbolic associations pride of place. 3) Uses preexisting visual or cultural materials.

The career of the painter Robert Rauschenberg (1925) may be used to illustrate this change of direction. Connected with Abstract Expressionism in his youth, Rauschenberg remained faithful throughout the course of his artistic career to certain principles of traditional modernism such as psychic automatism. *Express* (Cat. 721) belongs to a group of paintings in which the elements enumerated above, and especially the last, can be appreciated for the first time in the work of the artist.

Among the stylistic precedents of Pop Art we could cite the free association of materials practised by the Dadaists, especially Schwitters (see Room 43). This Dadaist tradition remained alive in the United States during the 1940s and 1950s in the work of artists such as Joseph Cornell (1903-1972). At the end of the 1950s art critics were talking about a Neodadaist tendency in which they included Rauschenberg. However, historic Dadaism was based on an essentially introspective attitude: the artist was asking himself questions about the nature of modern art; for the Pop artist, in contrast, modern art was already a given fact, and what he asked himself questions about was the nature of the times in which he was living. A certain ideological Futurism may thus be identified in Pop Art, a tradition which has been expressed over the course of the 20th century in the exaltation of the mechanical and impersonal in modern life. The late painting of Léger and Stuart Davis (1894-1964) in the United States could be cited as examples. The two works by the latter artist in Room 48, and especially the later one, *Pochade* (Cat. 514), allow the plausibility of this hypothesis to be visually verified. While Stuart Davis is an example of a career which starts out from the synthesis of modernity and develops towards a Pop sensibility, Richard Lindner (1901-1978) illustrates a different line of development. Born in Germany and a graphic artist by profession, Lindner experienced the final stages of Expressionism and New Objectivity at close hand in the 1930s. This experience and the influence of Léger contributed to modelling his personal vision of American culture.

Along with the diversity of the roads to Pop Art we could mention that of those leading away from it. Ronald B. Kitaj (1932) and David Hockney (1937) were members of the London group in

721. **Robert Rauschenberg**
Express, 1963

Oil on canvas with silkscreen. 183 x 305 cm.

which the label Pop Art was generated. However, both of them avoided using the characteristic iconography of the first stage of the movement and evolved towards a figurative painting with a narrative character which was, especially in the case of Kitaj, strongly literary.

In any case, despite its stylistic dispersion, it is undoubtable that Pop Art will always primarily evoke the iconography drawn from the mass media, and it is also undoubtable that the international impact of a series of paintings done by Roy Lichtenstein (1923) as from 1962 contributed decisively to this historical association. In declarations made in 1963 the artist said that in painting images from comic strips the only thing that interested him was, like Ingres when he did his portraits, the drawing and the colour. *Woman in Bath* (Cat. 648) is one of the most beautiful paintings from this, Lichtenstein's classic period. The fact we can admire its beauty in terms of drawing and colour (as in the case of Mondrian, Léger, Picasso or Matisse)

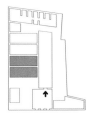

reveals a paradox. We recognise a masterpiece through its historical impact, its capacity to stamp a new direction on the art of its time different from that of the masterpieces of the past. At the same time, we recognise it as a masterpiece because we are moved to admire it, along with them, as a timeless work. The deep conviction that these two apparently contradictory manners of judging a work of art are at bottom the same thing is the key of aesthetic experience and the *raison d'être* of museums and art history.

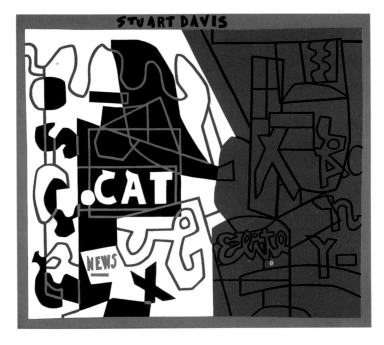

514. **Stuart Davis**
Pochade, 1958

Oil on canvas. 130 x 152 cm.

648. Roy Lichtenstein
A Woman in Bath, 1963

Oil on canvas. 171 x 171 cm.

LIST OF WORKS

EARLY ITALIANS
ROOM 1

70. BULGARINO, Bartolomeo. *Madonna and Child enthroned with a female martyr, Saint John the Baptist and four Angels,* c. 1340-1345 Tempera on panel, 48 x 26 cm.

123. DADDI, Bernardo. *The Crucifixion,* c. 1330-1335. Tempera on panel, 37.4 x 22.2 cm.

133. DUCCIO DI BUONINSEGNA. *Christ and the Samaritan Woman,* 1310-1311. Tempera on panel on gold background, 43.5 x 46 cm.

151. GADDI, Agnolo. *The Crucifixion,* c. 1390. Tempera on panel, 32.5 x 30.3 cm.

161. GIOVANNI DI PAOLO. *Madonna of Humility,* c. 1440. Tempera on panel, 32.5 x 22.5 cm.

162. GIOVANNI DI PAOLO. *St Catherine before the Pope at Avignon,* early 1460s. Tempera on panel, 29 x 29 cm.

228.a-c. LORENZO VENEZIANO. *Portable Altarpiece with Crucifixion,* c.1370-1375. Tempera on panel, central panel: 83.6 x 30.7 cm; wings: 83 x 15 cm.

231. LUCA DI TOMME. *Adoration of the Magi,* c. 1360-1365. Tempera on panel, 41 x 42 cm.

247. MASTER OF 1355. *Coronation of the Virgin with five Angels,* 1355. Tempera and gold on panel, 86 x 52.5 cm.

256. MASTER OF THE MAGDALEN. *Madonna and Child enthroned with Saint Dominic,Saint Martin and two Angels,* c. 1290 Tempera on a gabled panel, 177 x 86.57 cm.

260. MASTER OF THE POMPOSA CHAPTERHOUSE. *The Crucifixion,* c. 1320. Tempera on panel, 29 x 20.5 cm.

424.a-c. MASTER, VENETIAN, C. 1300-1310. *Madonna and Child Triptych.* Tempera on panel, central panel: 80 x 51 cm.; wings: 76.8 x 25.5 cm.

257. MASTER, VENETIAN, C. 1360. *Madonna of Humility with Angels and a Donor,* c.1360. Tempera on panel, 68.8 x 56.7 cm.

412. UGOLINO DI NERIO. *Christ on the Cross between the Virgin and Saint John,* c. 1330-1335 Tempera on panel, 134 (lower height 95 cm) x 90 x 4 cm.

425. VITALE DA BOLOGNA *The Crucifixion,* c. 1335. Tempera on panel, 93 x 51.2 cm.

SCULPTURES

S 44. *Virgin and Child,* , c. 1250. Polycaromed poplar, Height: 115.5 cm. Umbria (?)

S 52. *Our Lady of the Annunciation; Madonna Annunziata,* 1360 - 1380. Painted and gilt wood with plaster of Paris, Height: 58.8 cm. Siena

FURNITURE.

M 17. BENEDETTO DI BINDO y tondos de TADDELO DI BARTOLO. *Cassone sienés,* 1411-1412. Wood with stucco decoration, Height: 66 cm. Siena

MEDIEVAL ART
ROOM 2

199. HUGUET Jaume (Circle of). *The Pilgrims Mass,.* Tempera and gold on panel, 83 x 72 cm.

210. KOERBECKE, Johann. *The Assumption of the Virgin,* shortly before 1457. Oil on panel, 93.1 x 54.2 cm.

233. MAELESSKIRCHER, Gabriel. *Saint Luke at his Desk with ais Symbol the Bull,* 1478. Oil on panel, 77 x 32.2 cm.

234. MAELESSKIRCHER, Gabriel. *Saint Matthew at his Desk with his Symbol the Angel,* 1478. Oil on panel, 77.4 x 32.2 cm.

235. MAELESSKIRCHER, Gabriel. *Saint John the Evangelist at his Desk with his Symbol the Eagle,.* 1478. Oil on panel. 77.2 x 32.2 cm.

236. MAELESSKIRCHER, Gabriel. *Saint Mark at his Desk with his Symbol the Lion,* 1478. Oil on panel, 77.1 x 32.2 cm.

237. MAELESSKIRCHER, Gabriel. *Saint Luke painting the Madonna,* 1478. Oil on panel, 77 x 32 cm.

238. MAELESSKIRCHER, Gabriel. *The Miracle of Saint Matthew taming the Dragon,* 1478. Oil on panel, 77.2 x 32.2 cm.

239. MAELESSKIRCHER, Gabriel. *The Miracle of the Host at the Tomb of Saint John the Evangelist,* 1478 Oil on panel, 77 x 32 cm.

240. MAELESSKIRCHER, Gabriel. *The Martyrdom of Saint Mark,* 1478. Oil on panel, 77.2 x 32.2 cm.

44.a-e. MASTER BERTRAM. *The Holy Visage of Christ Triptych,* 1395 - 1410. Oil on panel, central panel: 30.8 x 24.2 cm.; wings: 30.8 x 12 cm.

246. MASTER OF THE VISION OF SAINT JOHN. *Saints Damian, Cosmas and Pantaleon,* c. 1455. Oil on panel, 130.5 x 72.2 cm.

245.a-c. MASTER, ANONYMOUS. *The Annunciation Triptych.* Mixed media on panel, central panel: 34.3 x 16.5 cm; wings: 34.3 x 8.5 cm.

268.a. MASTER, ANONYMOUS. *The Descent from the Cross,* c. 1420. Oil on panel, 62 x 30 cm.

272. MASTER, ANONYMOUS. *The Virgin and Child in the 'hortus conclusus',* c. 1410. panel, 28.6 x 18.5 cm.

273. MASTER, ANONYMOUS. *The Crucifixion with the 'Living Cross',* c. 1410. panel, 28.5 x 18.5 cm.

282. MATES, Joan. *Saint John the Evangelist and Saint John the Baptist with Donor,.* c. 1410. Oil on panel, 191 x 121 cm.

SCULPTURE

S 45. *Lion of St. Mark,* 13th century. Marble, Height: 38.8 cm. Southern Italy

Vitrine 1

Ivory

E 3. *The Baptism of Christ,* c. 1100. Ivory, Height: 15.9 cm. Campania

E 4. *Virgin and Child,* c. 1320 - 1330. Ivory, Height: 23.3 cm. Paris,

E 5. *Triptych with the Passion of Christ,* c. 1330. Ivory, Height: 24.6 cm. Paris,

E 6. *Diptych,* c. 1350. Ivory, Height: 17.8 cm. Paris

E 7. *Diptych with the Crucifixion and the Coronation of the Virgin,* 1350-1400. Ivory, Height: 11.5 cm. Paris

E 8. *Diptych,* 1350-1400. Ivory, Height: 16.6 cm. Cologne

K 91 I.1-7. *Seven Roundels,* c. 1400. Polychromed ivory "plaques ajourees", diam: 2.3 cm

E 10. *Virgin and Child,* c. 980-1000. Ivory, Height: 15.2 cm. Constantinople

EARLY NETHERLANDISH PAINTING ROOM 3

60. BOUTS, Dieric (Follower of). Virgin and Child, c. 1465. Oil on panel, 28.5 x 20 cm.

121. CHRISTUS, Petrus. *Our Lady of the Dry Tree,* c. 1450. Oil on panel, 17.4 x 12.3 cm.

124. DARET, Jacques. *The Nativity,* 1434-35. Oil on panel, 60 x 53 cm.

125. DAVID, Gerard. *The Crucifixion.* Oil on planed panel, 88 x 56 cm.

137.a-b. EYCK, Jan van. *The Annunciation Diptych,* c.1435-1441. Oil on panel, each panel: 39 x 24 cm.

142. FLANDES, Juan de. *The Lamentation,* c. 1500. Oil on panel, 23 x 30 cm.

251.a. MASTER OF MAGDALENE LEGEND (Attributed to). *Portrait of a Man as Saint Andrew,* c. 1480. Oil on panel, 28.2 x 19.7 cm.

261. MASTER OF SAINT GUDULE. *Clothing the Naked,* c. 1470. Oil on panel, 63.5 x 41.5 cm.

255. MASTER OF THE ANDRE MADONNA. *Madonna Standing in an Arch,* c. 1500. Oil on panel, 62 x 31 cm.

252.a-e. MASTER OF THE SAINT LUCY LEGEND. *Lamentation Triptych,* c. 1475. Oil on panel, central panel: 75 x 61 cm.; wings 75 x 27 cm.

253. MASTER OF THE SAINT URSULA LEGEND. *Virgin and Child with Two Angels,* c. 1480. Oil on uncradled panel, 36.6 x 27 cm.

269. MASTER OF THE VIRGO INTER VIRGINES. *The Crucifixion,* c. 1487. Oil on panel, 78 x 58.5 cm.

270. MASTER OF THE VIRGO INTER VIRGINES (Follower of). *The Last Supper.* Oil on panel, 69.7 x 38 cm.

435. WEYDEN, Rogier van der. *Madonna Enthroned,* c. 1433. Oil on panel, 14 x 10.5 cm.

SCULPTURES

S 57. Anna Selbdritt group, c. 1480-1500. *Oak, remains of old* (?) *polychromy,* Height: 100 cm

South Netherlandish

Vitrine 2

Reliquaries

E 1. *Eucharistic Dove,* c. 1210. Copper and champleve enamel, Height: 21.5 cm. Limoges

E 2. *Head of a Crozier Showing St. Michael and the Dragon,* 1225-1250. Copper and champleve enamel, Height:18.4 cm. Limoges

O 32. *Head Reliquary,* 1200-1400. Silver, with remains of gilding, Height: 26 cm.

E 33. *Reliquary Monstrance,* c. 1200-1250. Copper, champleve enamel, and rock crystal, Height: 28 cm

S 54. *Reliquary Bust,* 1350-1370. Polychromed walnut; Height: 47.6 cm. Cologne

THE QUATTROCENTO ITALIAN ART ROOM 4

53. BONFIGLIO, Benedetto di (or BONFIGLI). *The Annunciation,* c. 1455. Gold and tempera on panel, 51 x 36.5 cm.

57. BOTTICINI, Francesco. *Saints Cecilia, Valerian, Tiburtius, and Female Donor.* Tempera on panel, 52 x 44.5 cm.

61. BRAMANTINO. *The Ressurrected Christ.* Oil on panel, 109 x 73 cm.

107. COSTA, Lorenzo. *Madonna and Child Enthroned,* c. 1495. Oil on panel, 49.5 x 36.5 cm.

168. GOZZOLI, Benozzo. *Saint Jerome and a Friar,* c. 1470 Tempera on panel, 22.3 x 43.5 cm.

94. MASTER, FRANCO-FLEMISH probably active in Naples. *The Crucifixion.* Tempera on panel, 44.8 x 34 cm.

411. PAOLO UCCELLO. *Christ on the Cross, the Virgin and three mourning Saints,* c. 1460-1465. Tempera on panel, 45 x 67 cm.

344. ROBERTI, Ercole de'. *The Argonauts Leaving Colchis,* c. 1480. panel, 35 x 26.5 cm.

410. TURA, Cosme. *Saint John the Baptist in Patmos,* c. 1470. Tempera on panel, 27 x 32 cm.

426. VIVARINI, Bartolomeo. *Saint John the Baptist,* c. 1475. Tempera and oil on panel, 48.5 x 33.5 cm.

446. ZOPPO *Saint Jerome in the Wilderness,* 1460 - 1470. Mixed media on panel, 39 x 29 cm.

FURNITURE

M 18. NEROCCIO DE' LANDI, BOTTEGA. *Cassone,* c. 1470-75 / Wood and gilt plaster, Height: 65 cm. Siena or Orvieto

TEXTILES

T 87. *Lamentation of Christ,* c. 1530. Wool, 97 x 206 cm. Italy

SCULPTURE

S 46. DI DUCCIO, Agostino 'workshop of). *Virgin and Child with four angels,* ca.1465-70. Stucco painted and originally parcel-gilt; Height: 83.5 cm

S 48. 1-2. DELLA ROBBIA, Andrea (Workshop of). *Two Adoring Angels,* c. 1510. Terracotta, partially glazed in polychrome, Height: 95.7 cm

THE ART OF PORTRAITURE

ROOM 5

18. ANTONELLO DA MESSINA. *Portrait of a Man,* c. 1475 - 1476. Mixed media on panel, 27.5 x 21 cm.

74. CAMPIN, Robert. *Portrait of a Stout Man (Robert de Masmines?),* c 1425(?). Oil on panel, 35.4 x 23.7 cm.

89. CLEVE, Joos van. *Self-Portrait,* c. 1519. Oil on panel, 38 x 27 cm.

105. COSSA, Francesco del. *Portrait of a Man,* 1472 - 1477. Oil on panel, 38.5 x 27.5 cm.

130. DOMENICO VENEZIANO. *Monk Holding Cross,* 1445-1448. Tempera on panel, 69 x 44 cm.

141. FLANDES, Juan de. *Portrait of an Infanta (Catherine of Aragon?),* c. 1496. Oil on canvas, 31.5 x 22 cm.

158. GHIRLANDAIO, Domenico. *Portrait of Giovanna Tornabuoni,* 1488. Mixed media on panel, 77 x 49 cm.

191. HOLBEIN, Hans the Younger. *Portrait of King Henry VIII,* c. 1534-36. Oil on panel, 28 x 20 cm.

11. MASTER, FRANCO-FLEMISH. *Portrait of Wenceslaus of Luxembourg, Duke of Brabant,* c. 1400-15. Oil on panel, 34.4 x 25.4 cm.

284.a-b. MEMLING, Hans. (a) *Young Man at Prayer,* c. 1485 (b)*Marian Flowerpiece,.* Oil on panel, 29 x 22.5 cm.

319. PIERO DELLA FRANCESCA. *Portrait of a Child (Guidobaldo Da Montefeltro?),* c. 1483. Tempera on panel, 41 x 27.5 cm.

372. SOLARIO, Andrea. *Portrait of a Young Man,* after 1490. Oil on panel, 29.5 x 26 cm.

436. WEYDEN, Rogier van der (Attributed to). *Portrait of a Man (Pierre de Beffrement, Comte de Charny?),* c. 1464. Oil on panel, 32 x 22.8 cm.

VILLAHERMOSA GALLERY

ROOM 6

55. BORDONE, Paris. *Portrait of a Young Lady,* c. 1540 - 1560. Oil on canvas, 103 x 83 cm.

64. BRONZINO, Agnolo. *Portrait of a Young Man as Saint Sebastian,* c. 1525-28. Oil on panel, 87 x 76.5 cm.

192. HOLBEIN, Hans the Younger (Attributed to). *Portrait of Thomas Cromwell.* Oil on panel, 11 cm. diam.

310. PALMA IL VECCHIO. *Portrait of a Young Woman ("La Bella"),* c. 1525. Oil on canvas, 95 x 80 cm.

330. RAFFAELLO. *Portrait of a Young Man (Alessandro de Medici?),* c. 1515. Oil on panel, 43.8 x 29 cm.

423. VERONESE. *Portrait of a Young Lady with Lapdog,* 1560-1570. Oil on canvas, 105 x 79 cm.

428. VOUET, Simon. *The Rape of Europa,* c. 1640. Oil on canvas, 179 x 141.5 cm.

448. ZURBARAN, Francisco de. *Santa Casilda,* c. 1640-1645. Oil on canvas, 171 x 107 cm.

Vitrine 3

Enamels

E 11. 1-2. REYMOND, Pierre. *Two Limoges Tazzas with Covers,* 16th century Enamel and copper, Height: 23 cm. Limoges

E 12. 1-2. REYMOND, Pierre. *Pair of Candleholders,* 16th century. Enamel and copper, Height: 24 cm. Limoges

E 13. REYMOND, Pierre. *Large Dish,* 16th century. Enamel and copper, Diameter: 40.5 cm. Limoges

E 14.1-2. REYMOND, Pierre. *Pair of Pitchers,* ca. 1580. Enamel, Height: 27 cm. Limoges

E 16. 1-2. *Two Small Dishes,* 16th century. Enamel, Diameter: 20 cm. Limoges

Vitrine nº 4

Jewelery

J 35. *Portrait Pendant,* c. 1570;. Oil on silver (or coppered silver); openwork gold, enamel; Height: 8.4 cm. Florence ?, Spain ?

J 36. *Pendant Depicting a Female Nude (Bust),* c. 1600. Chalcedony, mounted in enamelled gold set with diamonds; Height: 9.7 cm. Spain (Mount); Italy or Spain (Bust)

J 37. *Talismanic Pendant,* c. 1550-1600. Ivory mounted in enamelled gold, set with pearls and a turquoise, Height 5.2 cm. Spain

J 38. *Reliquary Pendant in the Form of a Crowned Heart,* c. 1600. Enamelled gold set with rubies, diamonds and hung with a pearl, Height: 9.5 cm. Spain

J 39. *Pendant Depicting the Christ Child,* late 17th century. Enamelled gold set with emeralds and hung with a pearl, Height: 5.2 cm.

J 40. *Hind Pendant,* c. 1570 Enamelled gold set with a pearl, gems, Height: 8.5 cm. Spain

J 41. *Pendant in the Form of an Eagle,* c. 1600. Enamelled gold set with emeralds, rubies and hung with pearls, Height: 6.4 cm. Spain ?

J 42. *Pendant Depicting the Miraculous Apparition of Saint James,* c. 1575. Carved agate mounted in enamelled gold and hung with a pearl, Diameter: 4.8 cm. Spain

J 43. *Pendant Representing the Personification of Faith,* c. 1600. Enamelled gold set with diamonds and hung with a pearl, Height: 8 cm. Spain

O 61. *Tankard,* c. 1550. Silver; chased and matted; gilt, Height: 17.5 cm. Nuremberg

Vitrines nº 5-8

Gold and Silver

O 62. *Coin Tankard,* c. 1575-1600 Silver, gilt, and parcel gilt , Height: 27.6 cm. Transylvania

O 63. BAIR, Melchior. *Standing Covered Beaker,* c. 1600. Silver, gilt, Height: 50 cm. Augsburg

O.64.REHLEIN, Martin. *Presentation Cup,* c. 1595 Silver, gilt?, Height: 55.7 cm. Nuremberg

O 65. *The Rakoczy Cup,* c. 1570-c. 1620. Silver, embossed, cast; chased, matted, engraving, hatching , Height: 56.8 cm. Augsburg and Nuremberg

O 66. STRAUB, Heinrich.*Covered Standing Cup,* 17th century / Silver, gilt, Height: 52 cm. Nuremberg

O 67. 1-2. *Double Standing Cup (Upper/Lower Cups),* c. 1570. Silver, embossed; chased, engraved and matted, Height: 58 cm. Augsburg

O 68. MYLIUS, Daniel Friedrich von. *Tankard.* Silver, parcel gilt, Height: 22 cm. Danzig

O 69. 1-2. *Double Standing Cup,* c. 1565. Silver, embossed; chased, etched and engraved; gilt, Height: 45 cm. Augsburg

O 70. *"Hanse" Tankard,* c. 1580. Silver; embossed; cast; gilt. Cast pewter. Height: 49 cm. Lubeck?

O 71. BRUSSELL, Wolf. *Coconut Cup Mounted in Silver-gilt,* c. 1550 Coconut; silver, embossed, chased, engraved, matted, Height: 29.1 cm. Nuremberg

O 72. LINDEN, Esias Zur. *Rhinoceros Cup,* c. 1610. Carved Chinese rhinoceros cup; Height: 17.1 cm. Nuremberg

O 73. *Display Cup of Carved Quartz,* c. 1560-1570. Quartz and Silver gilt, Height: 25 cm. Antwerp

O 74. HARDERS, Claus. *Decorative Turbo Shell Cup,* late 16th Century. Turbo shell silver, gilt, Height: 19.5 cm. Luneburg

O 75. FLORIS. Cornelius. *Nautilus Cup,* c. 1577. Nautilus shell with silver-gilt mounts, Height: 32 cm. Delf

O 76. BELLEKIN, Cornelius. *Nautilus Cup,* 1650-1675 y 1710-1720. Nautilus shell and silver, gilt, Height: 28.8 cm. Augsburg?

O 77. 1-2. *Double Standing Cup,* late 16th century Silver-gilt, Height: 38 cm. Nurenberg

O 78. *Coconut Cup Depicting the "Creation of Eve",* c. 1570. Coconut, incised; silver mounts, cast, chased, matted, Height: 32.7cm. Germany

O 79. VAN LEEUVEN, Tymen. *Ciborium, 1661.* Silver-gilt, Height: 52 cm. Utrecht

O 80. SCHENAUER, Jacob. *Tazza,* c. 1585. Silver gilt, Height: 52 cm.

O 81. MORINGER, Veit. *Covered Standing Cup,* c. 1555-1560 Silver; cast, chased and matted; gilt; gemstones, Height: 35 cm. Nuremberg

O 82. PETZOLT, Hans. *The Imhoff Standing Cup,* 1626 / Silver, gilt,Height: 46.3 cm. Nuremberg

O 83. GELB, Melchior. *Bellarmine (Bartmannskrug),* c. 1625. Silver and parcel-gilt, Height: 25.8 cm. Augsburg

FURNITURE

M 19. *Cassone,* c. 1500. Wood and gilding, Height: 58 cm. Tuscany

M 20. *Cassone with Legs in the form of Lion's Feet,* early 16th century. Walnut inlaid with light beech, Height: 68 cm. Florence

M 21. *Cassone with Carved, Relief Decoration (Figural),* 2ª half of 16th century. Walnut, Height: 76 cm. Rome

M 22 1-4. *Set of Four Hall/Side Chairs,* 1500-1550. Walnut and gilding, Height: 102 cm. Florence

M 23 1-4. *Set of Four Hall Chairs,* early 16th century. Walnut, Height: 98 cm. Florence

M 25. *Trunk/Cassone,* c. 1570 Chestnut, painted, Height: 49 cm. Venice

M 29. *Cassone,* c. 1560. Walnut and gilding, Height: 55 cm. Central Italy

TEXTILES AND CARPETS

T 88. *Jeziorak Vase Carpet (Figdor Vase Carpet),* 2nd half 17th century. Wool, cotton, and silk, 269 x 174 cm. Persia

T 89. *Figdor Silk Kileem (Kilim),* late 16th - early 17th century. Silk, metal-wrapped silk, and cotton, 194 x 124 cm. Persia

T 90. *Aynard Prayer Rug (Mughal),* 2nd quarter 17th century "Pashmine" wool-cashmere and silk, 124.5 x 90 cm. India

T 91. *Braganza Carpet,* c. 1650. Cotton and wool, 990 x 358 cm Persia. *Exhibited in Main Hall

T 92. *Van Pannwitz Medallion and Animal Carpet,* 16th century. Silk, wool, and cotton, 224 x 165 cm. Persia

T 86. *Tapestry Depicting Three Men Hunting a Falcon,* c. 1500. Wool, 278 x 349 cm. Burgundy. * Exhibited in Main Hall

SCULPTURES

S 47 RICCIO, called. *Virgin and Child,* c. 1520-1525. Terracotta, traces of polychromy, Height: 64.4 cm

S 49. DELLA ROBBIA, Andrea. *Saint Augustine,* c. 1490/ Terracotta glazed in polychrome, Diameter: 75.3 cm.

S 50. 1-2. SANSOVINO, called. *The Annunciation,* c. 1535. Terracotta, painted in polychrome, Height: 85 cm. y 89.7 cm.

ITALIAN PAINTING OF THE 16TH CENTURY

ROOM 7

20. ASPERTINI, Amico. *Portrait of Tommaso Raimondi,* c. 1500. Oil on panel, 41.5 x 32.5 cm.

29. BARTOLOMEO, Fra. *Holy Family with Infant Saint John,* c. 1506-1507. Oil on panel, 62 x 47 cm.

30. BARTOLOMMEO VENETO. *Portrait of a Man,* 1525-1530. Oil on panel, 87.3 x 59 cm.

33. BECCAFUMI, Domenico. *Madonna and Child with St. John and St. Jerome,* c. 1523-1524. Oil on panel, diameter: 85.5 cm.

38. BELLINI, Gentile. *The Annunciation,* c. 1465. Tempera and oil on panel, 133 x 124 cm.

39. BELLINI, Giovanni. *Nunc Dimittis.* 1505-1510. Oil on panel, 62 x 82.5 cm.

52. BOLTRAFFIO, Giovanni Antonio. *Portrait of a Lady as Saint Lucy,* c. 1500. Oil on panel, 51.5 x 36.5 cm.

63. BRONZINO, Agnolo. *Cosimo de Medici in Armour.* Oil on panel, 76.5 x 59 cm.

82. CARPACCIO, Vittore. *Young Knight in a Landscape,* 1510. Oil on canvas, 218.5 x 151.5 cm.

145. FOSCHI, Pierfrancesco di Jacopo. *Portrait of a Lady,* 1530-1535. Oil on panel, 101 x 79 cm.

159. GHIRLANDAIO, Ridolfo. *Portrait of a Nobleman of the Capponi Family.* Oil on panel, 80 x 60.5 cm.

230. LOTTO, Lorenzo. *Self-Portrait.* Oil on panel, 43 x 35 cm.

232. LUINI, Bernardino. *Virgin and Child with the Infant Saint John,* 1523-1525. Oil on canvas, 86 x 60 cm.

309. PALMA IL VECCHIO. *Sacra Conversazione,* 1515-1520. Oil on canvas, 105 x 136 cm.

320. PIERO DI COSIMO. *Madonna and Child with Angels,* 1500-1510. panel, diam. 78 cm.

369. SEBASTIANO DEL PIOMBO. *Portrait of Ferry Carondolet with his Secretaries,* 1510-1512. Oil on panel, 112.5 x 87 cm.

405. TIZIANO. *Portrait of Doge Francesco Vernier,* 1554-1556. Oil on canvas, 113 x 99 cm.

GERMAN PAINTING OF THE 16TH CENTURY

ROOM 8

22. BAEGERT, Derick. *The Good Centurion and other men beneath the Cross,* 1477-1478. Oil on panel, 81.5 x 51 cm.

23. BAEGERT, Derick. *A group of figures with Saint Veronica holding the Sudarium,* 1477-1478 Oil on panel, 113 x 97.5 cm.

24. BAEGERT, Derick. *Christ carrying the Cross, with four horsemen in the foreground,* 1477-1478. Oil on panel, 87 x 98 cm.

25. BAEGERT, Derick. *The Kneeling Magdalen,* 1477-1478. Oil on panel, 80 x 42.3 cm.

26. BAEGERT, Derick. *A group of men on Mount Calvary,* 1477-1478. Oil on panel, 159 x 92.3 cm.

67. BRUYN, Barthel the Elder. *Portrait of a Man of the Patrician Family of Weinsberg,* Cologne, c. 1538-1539. Oil on panel, 35 x 25.5 cm.

68. BRUYN, Barthel the Elder. *Portrait of a Woman,* c. 1538-1539. Oil on panel, 34.9 x 25.5 cm.

69. BRUYN, Barthel the Elder. *The Nativity,* c. 1520. Oil on panel, 62.5 x 55.5 cm.

71. BURGKMAIR, Hans. *Christ carried to the Tomb,* c. 1520. Oil on panel, 66.3 x 118.3 cm.

114. CRANACH, Lucas the Elder. *The Virgin with Child eating Grapes,* c. 1509-1510. Oil on panel, 71.5 x 44.2 cm.

134. DÜRER, Albrecht. *Jesus Among the Doctors,* 1506. Oil on panel, 64.3 x 80.3 cm.

212.a-c. KULMBACH, Hans Suess von. *Rosary Triptych.* Oil on panel. Central panel: 117.2 x 84.3 cm., shortly before 1510. Wings: 122.5 x 37.8 cm. y 122 x 38.5 cm., 1513

250. MASTER OF GROSSGMAIN. *Saint Jerome,* 1498. Oil on panel, 67 x 49 cm; framed: 81 x 64 x 4 cm.

259. MASTER, ANONYMOUS. *Four scenes from the Passion,* c. 1495-1500. Oil on panel, 163.8 x 55.5 cm.

264. MASTER, ANONYMOUS. *Portrait of a Woman,* c. 1480. Oil on panel, 50.4 x 39.2 cm.

265. MASTER, ANONYMOUS. *Portrait of a Man,* c. 1480. Oil on panel, 55 x 43.5 cm.

308. PACHER, Michael (Follower of). *Madonna with Saint Margaret and Saint Catherine,* c. 1500. Oil on panel, 166 x 76.5 cm.

380. STRIGEL, Bernhard. *The Annunciation to Saint Anne,* c. 1505-1510. Oil on panel, 58 x 30 cm.

382. STRUEB, Hans and/or Jakob. *The Visitation,* c. 1505. Oil on panel, 80 x 55.7 cm.

SCULPTURES

S 55. *Coronation of the Virgin,* c. 1520 -1530. Limewood, old polychromy and overpainting, Height: 143 cm. Austria

S 56. Master of the Wettringen Altar (attrib.to), workshop Tilmann Riemenscheider. *Lamentation for the Dead Christ,* c. 1505 - 1510. Limewood, probably originally polychromed, Height: 91 cm.

ROOM 9

2. ALTDORFER, Albrecht. *Portrait of a Woman,* 1522 (?). Oil on panel, 59 x 45 cm.

4. AMBERGER, Christoph. *Portrait of Matthäus Schwarz,* 1542. Oil on panel, 73.5 x 61 cm.

27. BALDUNG GRIEN, Hans. *Adam and Eve,* 1531. Oil on panel, 147.5 x 67.3 cm.

28. BALDUNG GRIEN, Hans. *Portrait of a Woman,* 1530(?). Oil on panel, 69.2 x 52.5 cm.

36. BEHAM, Barthel. *Portrait of Ruprecht Stüpf,* 1528. Oil on panel, 67.3 x 50.3 cm.

37. BEHAM, Barthel. *Portrait of Ursula Rudolph, Wife of Ruprecht Stüpf,* 1528. Oil on panel, 67.3 x 50.3 cm.

271.a. BEURER, Wolfgang. *Portrait of a Man,* 1487. Oil on panel, 37.3 x 27.5 cm.

244. BREU, Jörg the Elder and an unknown painter. *Portrait of Coloman Helmschmid and his Wife Agnes Breu,* c. 1500-1505 Oil on lime panel, 38 x 47.9 cm.

92. CLOUET, François. *Le Billet Doux,* c. 1570. Oil on paper on panel, 41.4 x 55 cm.

108. CRANACH, Hans. *Hercules at the Court of Omphale,* 1537. Oil on panel, 57.5 x 85.3 cm.

109. CRANACH, Hans. *Portrait of a Bearded Man,* 1534. Oil on panel, 51.4 x 35.1 cm.

113. CRANACH, Lucas The Younger. *Portrait of a Woman,* 1539. Oil on panel, 61.5 x 42.2 cm.

112. CRANACH, Lucas the Elder. *Portrait of the Emperor Charles V,* 1533. Oil on panel, 51.2 x 36 cm.

115. CRANACH, Lucas the Elder. *Reclining Nymph*, c. 1530-34. Oil on panel, 75 x 120 cm.

189. HOLBEIN, Hans the Elder. *Portrait of a Young Woman in Profile*, c. 1518-1520. Oil on panel, 23.6 x 17 cm.

190. HOLBEIN, Hans the Elder. *Portrait of a Man*, c. 1518-1520. Oil on panel, 23.7 x 17 cm.

275. MALER, Hans. *Portrait of Anne of Hungary and Bohemia*, 1519. Oil on panel, 44 x 33.3 cm.

254. MASTER OF THE LÜNEBURG LAST JUDGEMENT. *Portrait of a Young Man*, c. 1485. Oil on panel, 62 x 38.5 cm.

54. MASTER, ANONYMOUS. *Portrait of a Woman wearing the Order of the Swan*, c. 1490. Oil on panel, 44.7 x 28.2 cm.

188. MASTER, ANONYMOUS. *Portrait of a Young Man*, c. 1525-1530. Oil on panel, 32 x 26 cm.

258. MASTER, ANONYMOUS of the School of Lucas Cranach the Elder. *Portrait of a Woman aged 26*, 1525. Oil on panel, 61.6 x 38.8 cm.

213. MONOGRAMMIST TK. *Portrait of a Man (Georg Thurzo?)*, 1518. Oil on panel, 45.5 x 33.5 cm.

214. MONOGRAMMIST TK. *Portrait of a Woman (Anna Fugger?)*, 1518. Oil on panel, 45.5 x 33.2 cm.

325. POLACK, Jan. *Portrait of a Benedictine Abbot*, 1484. Oil on panel, 57.3 x 41 cm.

366. SCHAFFNER, Martin. *Portrait of a Man*, c. 1515. Oil on panel, 35.5 x 25.5 cm.

379. STRIGEL, Bernhard. *Portrait of a Man*, 1528(?). Oil on panel. 42.9 x 30.3 cm.

408. TRAUT, Wolf. *Portrait of a Woman*, 1510. Oil on panel, 37.5 x 28.5 cm.

434. WERTINGER, Hans. *Portrait of the 'Knight Christoph'*, 1515. Oil on panel, 113 x 61.5 cm.

440. WOLGEMUT, Michael. *Portrait of Levinus Memminger*, c. 1485. Oil on panel, 33.7 x 22.9 cm.

443. ZEHENDER, Gabriel. *Portrait of a Married Couple*, 1525. Oil on panel, 40.9 x 51.5 cm.

NETHERLANDISH PAINTING OF THE 16TH CENTURY

ROOM 10

34. BEER, Jan de. *The Birth of the Virgin*, c. 1520. Oil on panel, 111.5 x 131 cm.

35. BEER, Jan de. *The Annunciation*, c. 1520. Oil on panel, 111.5 x 131 cm.

41. BENSON, Ambrosius. *Gentleman at Prayer*, c. 1525. Oil on panel, 35.5 x 26 cm.

90. CLEVE, Joos van. *Infant Saviour on Winged Orb*, c. 1530. Oil on panel, 37 x 26 cm.

93. COCK, Jan Wellen de. *The Temptation of Saint Anthony*, c. 1520. Oil on panel, 60 x 45.5 cm.

100. CORNEILLE DE LYON. *Portrait of Robert de la Marck*, c. 1535. Oil on panel, 18.5 x 15.5 cm.

101. CORNELISZ, Jacob van Oostsanen. *Portrait of a Lady (Queen Isabella of Denmark?)*, c. 1524. Oil on panel, 33 x 23 cm.

163. GOSSAERT, Jan. *Adam and Eve*, c.1507-1508. Oil on panel, 56.5 x 37 cm. rounded top

183. HEEMSKERCK, Maerten van. *Portrait of a Lady with Spindle and Distaff*, c. 1531. Oil on panel, 105 x 86 cm.

220. LEYDEN, Aertgen van. *Portrait of a Donor*, c. 1530 (?). Oil on panel, 25.5 x 22 cm.

221. LEYDEN, Lucas van (after). *The Cardplayers*, c. 1520. Oil on panel, 29.8 x 39.5 cm.

249. MASTER OF FRANKFURT. *The Holy Family*, c. 1508. Oil on panel, 76 x 57 cm.

10. MASTER, ANONYMOUS. *Rest on the Flight into Egypt*, c. 1540. Oil on panel, 43.5 x 29.5 cm.

14. MASTER, ANONYMOUS. *Saint Paul*, 1525. Oil on panel, 44 x 21 cm.

13. MASTER, ANONYMOUS NETHERLANDISH. *Madonna and Nursing Child*, c. 1525. Watercolor and gold on fine canvas, 39.7 x 29.7 cm.

9. MASTER, FLEMISH. *Standing Madonna and Child in Triumphal Setting*, c. 1530. Oil on panel, 27.7 x 20.2 cm.

293. MOSTAERT, Jan. *Kneeling Female Donor with Redeemed of the Old Testament*, c. 1520. Oil on panel, 24 x 16 cm.

294. MOSTAERT, Jan. *The Banishment of Hagar*. Oil on panel, 94 x 131 cm.

305. ORLEY, Bernaert van. *The Rest on the Flight into Egypt*, c. 1515. Oil on panel, 87.5 x 72.2 cm.

314. PATINIR, Joachim. *Landscape with the Rest on the Flight into Egypt*, c. 1515-1516. Oil on panel, 31.5 x 57.5 cm.

328. PROVOST, Jan. *Portrait of a Female Donor*, c. 1505. Oil on panel, 53.5 x 46 cm.

332. REYMERSWAELE, Marinus van. *The Calling of Saint Matthew*, c. 1530. Oil on panel, 70.6 x 88 cm.

368. SCOREL, Jan van. *Madonna of the Daffodils with Donors,* c. 1535 (?). Oil on panel, 55.5 x 76.2 cm.

414. VALCKENBORCH, Lucas van (?). *The Massacre of the Innocents,* 1586. Oil on oak panel, 76.6 x 108.1 cm.

TITIAN, TINTORETTO, BASSANO, EL GRECO
ROOM 11

31. BASSANO, Jacopo. *Pastoral Landscape,* c. 1560. Oil on canvas, 139 x 129 cm.

169. GRECO, EL. *Christ with the Cross,* 1602-1607. Oil on canvas, 66 x 52.5 cm.

170. GRECO, El. *The Immaculate Conception,* 1607-1613. Oil on canvas, 108 x 82 cm.

171. GRECO, EL. *Annunciation,* 1596-1600. Oil on canvas, 114 x 67 cm.

172. GRECO, EL. *Annunciation,* 1567-1577. Oil on canvas, 117 x 98 cm.

17. MASTER, VENETIAN. *The Last Supper,* c. 1570. Oil on canvas, 121 x 190 cm.

401. TINTORETTO. *The Meeting of Tamar and Juda,* c. 1555-58. Oil on canvas, 150 x 155 cm.

402. TINTORETTO. *Annunciation to the Wife of Manoah,* c. 1555-58. Oil on canvas, 150 x 155 cm.

406. TIZIANO. *Saint Jerome in the Wilderness,* c. 1575. Oil on canvas, 135 x 96 cm.

EARLY BAROQUE. CARAVAGGIO AND BERNINI
ROOM 12

347. BABUREN, Dirck Jaspersz. van (?). *Saint Sebastian Tended by Saint Irene and her Maid,* c. 1615. Oil on canvas, 169 x 128 cm.

81. CARAVAGGIO. *Saint Catherine of Alexandria,* c. 1597. Oil on canvas, 173 x 133 cm.

155. GENTILESCHI, Orazio. *Lot and His Daughters,* c. 1621-1623. Oil on canvas, 120 x 168.5 cm.

335. RIBERA, Jusepe de. *The Penitent Saint Jerome,* 1634. Oil on canvas, 78 x 126 cm.

336. RIBERA, Jusepe de. *Lamentation over the Body of Christ,* 1633. Oil on canvas, 157 x 210 cm.

415. VALENTIN DE BOULOGNE. *David With the Head of Goliath and Two Soldiers,* 1620-1622. Oil on canvas, 99 x 134 cm.

SCULPTURES

S 51. *Saint Sebastian,* 1615 BERNINI, Giovanni Lorenzo. Marble, Height: 98.8 cm.

THE BAROQUE IN THE 17TH CENTURY
ROOM 13

59. BOURDON, Sebastien. *The Holy Family, With Saint Elisabeth and Saint John the Baptist,* c. 1660-1670. Oil on canvas, 39 x 50 cm.

226. CLAUDE LORRAIN. *Pastoral Landscape with a Flight into Egypt,* 1663. Oil on canvas, 193 x 147 cm.

139. FETTI, Domenico. *The Good Samaritan,* 1610-1623. Oil on panel, 59.6 x 43.7 cm.

140. FETTI, Domenico. *The Parable of the Sower,* 1610-1623. Oil on panel, 61 x 44.5 cm.

218. LE NAIN, Antoine. *The Young Musicians,* c. 1640. Oil on copper, 19.5 x 25.5 cm.

287. MOLA, Pier Francesco. *Saint John the Baptist Preaching in the Wilderness,* c. 1650-1655. Oil on canvas, 73.5 x 99 cm.

363. SALINI, Tommaso. *Young Peasant with Flask,* c. 1610. Oil on canvas, 99 x 73 cm.

ROOM 14

160. GHISLANDI, Fra Vittore, *Portrait of a Jeweller.* Oil on canvas, 73 x 57 cm.

A 807. GIORDANO, Luca. *The Judgement of Solomon.* Oil on canvas, 250.8 x 308 cm.

327. PRETI, Mattia. *A Concert,* c. 1630-1640. Oil on canvas, 107 x 145 cm.

A 822. PRETI, Mattia. *The Liberation of Saint Peter,* c. 1645. Oil on canvas, 145.5 x 197.5 cm.

381. STROZZI, Bernardo. *Saint Cecilia,* 1623-1625. Oil on canvas, 150 x 110 cm.

ROOM 15

129. DOLCI, Carlo. *The Young Jesus with a Wreath of Flowers,* 1663. Oil on canvas, 103 x 71 cm.

176. GUERCINO. *Christ and the Samaritan Woman at the Well,* 1640-1641. Oil on canvas, 116 x 156 cm.

278. MARATTA, Carlo. *Saint Mark, c. 1670. Oil on canvas,* 101 x 74.5 cm.

296. MURILLO, Bartolome Esteban. *Madonna and Child with Saint Rosalina of Palermo,* c. 1670. Oil on canvas, 190 x 147 cm.

A 820. MURILLO, Bartolomé Esteban. *Saint Francis in Ecstasy*, c. 1650-1655 Oil on canvas, 168.7 x 113 cm.

A 825. SOMER, Hendrik van. *Lot and his Daughters*. Oil on canvas, 148.5 x 194.5 cm.

ITALIAN PAINTING OF THE 18TH CENTURY

ROOM 16

A 802. CANALETTO. *View of San Giovanni e Paolo*, Venice. Oil on canvas 42 x 32.5 cm.

A 803. CANALETTO. *Capriccio view of a Palace Interior*, 1765. Oil on canvas, 42 x 32.5 cm.

311. PANINI, Gian Paolo. *The Expulsion from the Temple*, 1724. Oil on canvas, 74 x 99 cm.

312. PANINI, Gian Paolo. *The Healing of the Sick*, c. 1724. Oil on canvas, 74 x 99 cm.

340. RICCI, Sebastiano. *Neptune and Amphitrite*, c. 1691-1694. Oil on canvas, 94 x 75 cm.

341. RICCI, Sebastiano. *Bacchus and Ariadne*, c. 1691-1694. Oil on canvas, 94 x 75 cm.

ROOM 17

40. BELLOTTO, Bernardo. *Capriccio Padovano*, c. 1740-1742. Oil on canvas, 48.5 x 73 cm.

45. CANALETTO. *View of Piazza San Marco, Venice*, before 1723. Oil on canvas, 141.5 x 204.5 cm.

76. CANALETTO. *View of Canal Grande from San Vio, Venice*, before 1723. Oil on canvas, 140.5 x 204.5 cm.

78. CANALETTO. *Warwick Castle, the South Front*, c. 1749. Oil on canvas, 75 x 120.5 cm.

174. GUARDI, Francesco. *View of Canal Grande with Santa Lucia and Santa Maria Di Nazareth*, c. 1780. Oil on canvas, 48 x 78 cm.

175. GUARDI, Francesco. *View of Canal Grande with San Simeone Piccolo and Santa Lucia*, c.1780. Oil on canvas, 48 x 78 cm.

281. MARIESCHI, Michele. *View of the Canal Grande with Santa Maria Della Salute*. Oil on canvas, 83.5 x 121 cm.

394. TIEPOLO, Giambattista. *The Death of Hyacinthus*, 1752-1753. Oil on canvas, 287 x 232 cm.

397. TIEPOLO, Giandomenico. *Apotheosis of Hercules*, c. 1765. Oil on canvas, 101.3 x 85.5 cm.

A 830. ZOCCHI, Giuseppe. *View of Florence and the Arno at Ponte Santa Trinita*. Oil on canvas, 57 x 87.5 cm.

ROOM 18

32. BATONI, Pompeo Girolamo. *Portrait of the Contessa Di S. Martino*, 1785. Oil on canvas, 99 x 74 cm.

87. CERUTI, Giacomo Il Pitocchetto. *Portrait of a Man*, c. 1750. Oil on canvas, 119.5 x 95.5 cm

88. CERUTI, Giacomo Il Pitocchetto. *Portrait of a Lady*, c. 1750. Oil on canvas, 119.5 x 95.5 cm.

116. CRESPI, Giuseppe Maria. *Portrait of Count Fulvio Crati*. Oil on canvas, 228 x 153 cm.

224. LONGHI, Pietro. *The Tickle*, c. 1755. Oil on canvas, 61 x 48 cm.

316. PIAZZETTA, Giovanni Battista. *Portrait of Giulia Lama*, c. 1715. Oil on canvas, 69.4 x 55.5 cm.

324. PITTONI, Giovanni Battista. *The Sacrifice of Polissena*, 1730-1740. Oil on canvas, 72 x 58 cm.

A 823. RICCI, Sebastiano. *Bethsheba At Her Bath*, 1728. Oil on canvas, 39 x 31.5 cm.

396. TIEPOLO, Giambattista. *The Death of Sophonisba*, c. 1755-60. Oil on canvas, 48.3 x 38.2 cm.

FLEMISH PAINTING OF THE 17TH CENTURY

ROOM 19

66. BRUEGHEL I, Jan. *Christ in the Storm on the Sea of Galilee*, 1596. Oil on beaten copper, 26.6 x 35 cm.

A 801. BRUEGHEL I, Jan. *The Garden of Eden*, c.1612. Oil on oak panel, 59.4 x 95.6 cm.

135. DYCK, Anthony van. *Portrait of Jacques Le Roy*, 1631. Oil on canvas, 117.8 x 100.6 cm.

206. KETEL, Cornelis. *Portrait of a Man aged 58*, 1594. Oil on oak panel, 83.2 x 65.8 cm.

207. KETEL, Cornelis. *Portrait of a Woman aged 56*, 1594. Oil on panel, 83 x 67.3 cm.

208. KEY, Adriaen Thomasz. *Willem I, Prince of Orange, called William the Silent*, 1579. Oil on panel, 45.3 x 32.8 cm.

288. MONOGRAMMIST 'IDM'. *View of a River Port with Castel Sant'Angelo, Rome*. Oil on oak panel, 50.2 x 94 cm.

289. MONOGRAMMIST 'IDM'. *View of a Village on a River*. Oil on oak panel, 49.8 x 94 cm.

291. MOR, Anthonis van Dashorst. *Giovanni Battista di Castaldo,* c. 1550. Oil on oak panel, 107.6 x 82.2 cm.

350. RUBENS, Peter Paul. *The Toilet of Venus,* after 1629. Oil on canvas, 137 x 111 cm.

351. RUBENS, Peter Paul. *The Blinding of Samson,* 1609-1610. Oil on oak panel, 37.5 x 58.5 cm.

352. RUBENS, Peter Paul. *Portrait of a Young Woman with a Rosary,* c. 1609-1610. Oil on oak panel, 107 x 76.7 cm.

348. RUBENS, Peter Paul (Workshop of (?)). *St Michael Expelling Lucifer and the Rebellious Angels from Heaven,* c. 1622. Oil on canvas, 149 x 126 cm.

388. TENIERS II, David and KESSEL, Jan van. *The Submission of the Sicilian Rebels to Antonio de Moncada in 1411,* 1663. Oil on rolled copper, 54 x 68.2 cm.

389. TENIERS II, David and KESSEL, Jan van. *The Presentation of the Captain General's Baton to Anatonio de Moncada by Queen Bianca, Regent of Sicily in 1410,* 1664. Oil on rolled copper, 54.5 x 68.9 cm.

427. VOS, Cornelis de. *Antonia Canis,* 1624. Oil on oak panel, 123.7 x 94.2 cm.

NETHERLANDISH PAINTING OF THE 17TH CENTURY: ITALIANATE TRENDS AND PORTRAITS
ROOM 20

62. BREENBERGH, Bartholomeus. *Capriccio View of a Mediterranean Port,* 1650. Oil on canvas, 115.6 x 88.7 cm.

393. BRUGGHEN, Hendrick ter. *Esau Selling His Birthright,* c. 1627. Oil on canvas, 106.7 x 138.8 cm.

136. EVERDINGEN, Cesar van. *Vertumnus and Pomona.* Oil on oak panel, 47.9 x 38.9 cm.

201. JORDAENS, Jacob (and Assistant(s). *The Holy Family with an Angel,* c. 1618-1628. Oil on canvas, 89.7 x 103 cm.

225. LOO, Jacob van. *Group of People Making Music,* ca. 1650. Oil on canvas, 73.3 x 66 cm.

375. STOM, Matthias. *The Supper at Emmaus,* c. 1633-1639. Oil on canvas, 111.8 x 152.4 cm.

384. SWEERTS, Michiel. *Soldiers Playing Dice,* c. 1656-1658. Oil on canvas, 86.7 x 74 cm.

385. SWEERTS, Michiel. *Boy in a Turban holding a Nosegay,* c. 1655. Oil on canvas, 76.4 x 61.8 cm.

A 827. VERKOLJE, Nicolas. The Finding of Moses. Oil on canvas, 99 x 115 cm.

442. WTEWAEL, Joachim Antonisz. The Holy Family with Saints and Angel, c. 1606-1610. Oil on copper, 19.8 x 15.5 cm.

ROOM 21

51. BOL, Ferdinand. *Young Man in a Feathered Cap,* c. 1647. Oil on canvas, 88.6 x 77 cm.

390. BORCH, Gerard ter. *Portrait of a Man Aged 42,* 1652. Oil on rolled copper, 24.1 x 19.3 cm.

391. BORCH, Gerard ter. *Portrait of a Woman Aged 30,* c. 1652. Oil on rolled copper, 23.9 x 18.9 cm.

392. BORCH, Gerard ter. *Portrait of a Man Reading a Coranto,* c. 1675. Oil on canvas, 48 x 39.5 cm.

143. FLINCK, Govert. *Portrait of a Man,* 1640. Oil on oak panel, 67.1 x 55.1 cm.

184. HELST, Bartholomeus van der. *Portrait of a Man at a Desk with Documents,* c. 1655. Oil on canvas, 105 x 88 cm.

186. HEYDEN, Jan Jansz. van der. *Interior of a Study,* c. 1710-1712. Oil on canvas, 77 x 63.5 cm.

209. KEYSER, Thomas Hendricksz. de. *Portrait of Two Women and a Boy,* 1632. Oil on oak panel, 70.2 x 50.2 cm.

242. MAES, Nicolaes. *Portrait of a Man,* c. 1666-1667. Oil on canvas, 91.4 x 72.7 cm.

243. MAES, Nicolaes. *Portrait of a Woman,* 1667. Oil on canvas, 91.7 x 72.4 cm.

286. MIERIS I, Frans van. *Portrait of a Woman with a Lap-Dog,* 1672. Oil on oak panel, 31.7 x 25.4 cm.

302. NETSCHER, Caspar. *Portrait of a Woman,* 1676. Oil on canvas, 54.2 x 44.7 cm.

301. NETSCHER, Caspar (Attributed to). *Portrait of a Man.* Oil on canvas, 54 x 45.4 cm.

331. REMBRANDT, Harmensz. van Rijn (Workshop or Follower of). *Portrait of Rembrandt van Rijn,* c. 1643. Oil on oak panel, 72 x 54.8 cm.

DUTCH PAINTING OF THE 17TH CENTURY. SCENES OF DAILY LIFE, INTERIORS AND LANDSCAPES
ROOM 22

73. BIJLERT, Jan Hermansz. van (Attributed to). *Young Man Playing a Lute,* c. 1625. Oil on canvas, 97.8 x 82.6 cm.

65. BROUWER, Adriaen (Attributed to). *Village Scene with Men Drinking,* c. 1631-1635. Oil on oak panel, 63 x 95.9 cm.

A 808. GOYEN, Jan Josephsz. van. *On the Beach at Scheveningen*, 1646. Oil on canvas, 92.1 x 108.3 cm.

179. HALS, Frans. *Family Group in a Landscape*, c. 1645-1648. Oil on canvas, 202 x 285 cm.

178. HALS, Frans (Attributed to). *Fisherman Playing the Violin*, c. 1630. Oil on canvas, 86.4 x 70 cm.

193. HONDECOETER, Melchior de. *Bird of Prey in a Poultry Yard*. Oil on canvas, 122 x 139 cm.

194. HONTHORST, Gerrit van. *Merry Violinist*, c. 1624. Oil on canvas, 83 x 68 cm.

211. KONINCK, Philips Aertsz. *Panoramic Landscape*, 1655. Oil on canvas, 83.4 x 127.5 cm.

ROOM 23

154. GELDER, Aert de. *Christ and the Woman Taken in Adultery*, 1683. Oil on canvas, 71.8 x 94 cm.

195. HOOCH, Pieter Hendricksz de. *Woman with Needlework and a Child*, c. 1662-1668. Oil on canvas, 54.6 x 45.1 cm.

196. HOOCH, Pieter Hendricksz de. *The Interior of the Burgomasters' Council Chamber in the Amsterdam Town Hall*, 1661-1670 Oil on canvas, 112.5 x 99 cm.

241. MAES, Nicolaes. *The Naughty Drummer*, c. 1655. Oil on canvas, 62 x 66.4 cm.

285. METSU, Gabriel. *The Cook*, c. 1657-1662. Oil on canvas, 40 x 33,7 cm.

298. NEEFFS I, Peeter. *Church Interior*, 1615-1616. Oil on oak panel, 39.3 x 58.8 cm.

306. OSTADE, Adriaen van. *Tavern Interior*, 1661. Oil on oak panel, 32.4 x 24.6 cm.

307. OSTADE, Isaack van. *Traveller at a Cottage Door*, 1649. Oil on oak panel, 48.3 x 39.4 cm.

374. STEEN, Jan Havicksz. (Attributed to). *Wedding Scene*, c. 1653. Oil on oak panel, 62.4 x 49.3 cm.

387. TENIERS II, David. *Smokers in an Interior*, c. 1637. Oil on oak panel, 39.4 x 37.3 cm.

386. TENIERS, David. *The Village Fest*, c. 1650. Oil on panel, 45 x 75 cm.

438. WITTE, Emanuel de. *The Old Fish Market on the Dam, Amsterdam*, c. 1650. Oil on oak panel, 55 x 44.8 cm.

439. WITTE, Emanuel de. *Church Interior*, 166[9?]. Oil on oak panel, 52.1 x 40.2 cm.

ROOM 24

329. BROUWER, Adriaen (Follower of). *Smoker*. Oil on oak panel, 19.6 x 16.1 cm.

80. CAPPELLE, Jan van de. *Winter Landscape*. Oil on oak panel, 41 x 42.2 cm.

132. DOU, Gerrit. *Young Woman with a Lighted Candle at a Window*, c. 1658-1665. Oil on oak panel, 26.7 x 19.5 cm.

144. FLINCK, Govert (Attributed to). *Landscape with a Farm and a Bridge*, c. 1640. Oil on oak panel, 40.7 x 53.5 cm.

222. LIEVENS, Jan. *Landscape with the Rest on the Flight into Egypt*, c. 1635. Oil on oak panel, 34.3 x 51.8 cm.

304. OCHTERVELT, Jacob Lucasz. *Oyster Eaters*, c. 1665-1669. Oil on oak panel, 47.6 x 37.7 cm.

326. POST, Frans Jansz. *View of the Ruins of Olinda, Brazil*, 1665. Oil on canvas, 79.8 x 111.4 cm.

A 821. POTTER, Paulus. *Dapple Grey in the Landscape*, 1649. Oil on panel, 27 x 23 cm.

371. SIBERECHTS, Joannes. *Ford*, c. 1672. Oil on canvas, 63.5 x 55.4 cm.

373. STEEN, Jan Havicksz. *Self-Portrait as a Lutenist*. c. 1652-65. Oil on oak panel, 55.3 x 43.8 cm.

A 826. STEEN, Jan Havicksz. *Tavern Scene*, after 1661. Oil on canvas, 44.3 x 36.8 cm.

417. VELDE, Adriaen van de. *Pastoral Scene*, 1563. Oil on canvas, 48.5 x 62.5 cm.

419. VERMEER II VAN HAARLEM, Jan. *View of Haarlem from the Dunes*, c. 1660-1670. Oil on canvas, 65.3 x 84 cm.

441. WOUWERMANS, Philips. *Horse by a River Bank*, before 1646. Oil on oak panel, 28.7 x 22.7 cm.

A 829. WOUWERMANS, Philips. *Falconers Passing a Farmhouse*, c. 1645-1650. Oil on oak panel, 41 x 58 cm.

ROOM 25

A 800. BERCKHEYDE, Gerrit Adriaensz & HUCHTENBURCH, Johan van (?). *The Amsterdam Town Hall from the Dam*, c. 1673-1697. Oil on canvas, 53.6 x 63 cm.

42. BERCKHEYDE Gerrit Adriaensz. *The Nieuwezijds Voorburgswal, Amsterdam*, 1686. Oil on canvas, 53.7 x 63.9 cm.

43. BERCKHEYDE, Gerrit Adriaensz. *The Binnenhof, The Hague*, c. 1690. Oil on canvas, 54.5 x 63.5 cm.

185. HEYDEN, Jan Jansz van der. *Crossroad in a Wood*. Oil on oak panel, 44.5 x 55.5 cm.

A 816. HEYDEN, Jan Jansz. van der. *Outside a Town Hall*. Oil on panel, 29.5 X 34.6 cm.

187. HOBBEMA, Meindert Lubbertsz. *Woodland Pond*, c. 1660. Oil on canvas, 68.9 x 90.2 cm.

299. NEER, Aert van der. *Moonlit Landscape with a Road Beside a Canal*, c. 1647-1650. Oil on oak panel, 35.6 x 65.5 cm.

300. NEER, Aert van der. *Wooded River Landscape*, c. 1645. Oil on oak panel, 41.6 x 60.3 cm.

360. RUYSDAEL, Salomon Jacobsz van. *River Landscape with Fishermen*, 1645. Oil on oak panel, 51.5 x 83.6 cm.

362. SAENREDAM, Pieter Jansz. *The West Front of the Mariakerk, Utrecht*, 1662. Oil on oak panel, 65.1 x 51.2 cm.

A 824. SAFTLEVEN, Herman. *Rhine Landscape*, 1663. Oil on copper, 15 x 23.8 cm.

365. SAVERY, Roelandt. *Mountain Landscape with a Castle*, 1609. Oil on oak panel, 45.6 x 63 cm.

370. SEGHERS, Hercules Pietersz. *Extensive Landscape with Armed Men*, c.1625-1635. Oil on canvas, 36.5 x 54.3 cm.

437. WIJNANTS, Jan. *Country House in a Wooded Landscape*, 1667. Oil on canvas, 65.3 x 52 cm.

ROOM 26

79. CAPPELLE, Jan van de. *Coast Scene with Numerous Vessels*, after 1652. Oil on canvas, 67.3 x 58 cm.

117. CUYP, Aelbert Jacobsz. *Evening Landscape*, after 1645. Oil on oak panel, 48.3 x 74.9 cm.

167. GOYEN, Jan Josephsz. van. *Winter Landscape with Figures on Ice*, 1643. Oil on oak panel, 39.6 x 60.7 cm.

354. RUISDAEL, Jacob Isaacksz van. *View of Naarden*, 1647. Oil on oak panel, 34.8 x 67 cm.

357. RUISDAEL, Jacob Isaacksz van. *Road through Grain Fields near the Zuider Zee*, c. 1660-62. Oil on canvas, 44.8 x 54.6 cm.

359. RUISDAEL, Jacob Isaacksz van. *Rough Sea with Sailing Vessels*, c. 1668. Oil on canvas, 50.1 x 62.5 cm.

355. RUISDAEL, Jacob Isaacksz van (Attributed to). *Bleaching Fields at Bloemendael, near Haarlem*. Oil on canvas, 34.5 x 42.3 cm.

356. RUISDAEL, Jacob Isaacksz van (Attributed to). *View Inland from the Coastal Dunes*, c. 1670. Oil on canvas, 52.7 x 66.7 cm.

358. RUISDAEL, Jacob Isaacksz van (and Assistants?). *Canal with Commercial Buildings in Winter*, c. 1670. Oil on canvas, 65.8 x 96.7 cm.

793. RUYSDAEL, Salomon Jacobsz van. *View of Alkmaar From the Sea*, c. 1650. Oil on oak panel, 36 x 32.5 cm.

418. VELDE II, Willem van de. *The Dutch Fleet in the Goeree Roads*, 1664. Oil on canvas, 69.5 x 97.8 cm.

A 828. VLIEGER, Simon de. *Thunderstorm off the Coast*, c. 1645-1650. Oil on oak panel, 41.6 x 55.2 cm.

STILL LIFES OF THE 17TH CENTURY
ROOM 27

1. AELST, Willem van. *Glass Vase with Branches bearing Fruit*, 1664. Oil on canvas, 67.3 x 52.1 cm.

21. AST, Balthasar van der. *Flowers in a Chinese Vase*, 1628. Oil on oak panel, 51.6 x 33.1 cm.

56. BOSSCHAERT I, Ambrosius. *Chinese Vase with Flowers*, 1607. Oil on rolled copper, 68.6 x 50.8 cm.

118. CHARDIN, Jean Baptiste Simeon. *Still Life with Jug and Copper Cauldron*, c. 1728-1730. Oil on canvas, 32.4 x 39.2 cm.

150. FYT, Jan. *Vase of Flowers and a Bunch of Asparagus*, c. 1650. Oil on canvas, 63.7 x 75.4 cm.

180. HAMEN Y LEON, Juan van der. *Still Life with porcelain and sweets*, c. 1627. Oil on canvas, 77 x 100 cm.

181. HEDA, Willem Claesz. *Still Life with Rummer, Silver Tazza, Pie and other Objects*, 1634. Oil on oak panel, 43.7 x 68.2 cm.

A 815. HEEM, Cornelis de. *Flowers in a Glass Vase*, c. 1657-1660. Oil on oak panel, 47.3 X 35.6 cm.

182. HEEM, Jan Davidsz de. *Flowers in a Glass Vase*, c. 1665. Oil on oak panel, 53.4 x 41 cm.

202. KALF, Willem. *Still Life with a Chinese Bowl, Nautilus Beaker, Rummer, Flute glass and other Objects*, 1660 Oil on canvas, 64.1 x 55.9 cm.

203. KALF, Willem. *Still Life with a Nautilus Cup and other Objects*, 1662. Oil on canvas, 79.4 x 67.3 cm.

204. KALF, Willem. *Still Life with a Chinese Porcelain Ewer, Dish and other Objects*, c. 1660. Oil on canvas, 111 x 84 cm.

223. LINARD, Jacques. *Chinese Bowl with Flowers*, 1640. Oil on canvas, 53.2 x 66 cm.

413. TRECK, Jan Jansz. (attributed to). *Wine-Glass Stand, Pewter Jug and other Objects.* Oil on canvas, 81.8 x 57.8 cm.

376. VELDE III, Jan Jansz van de (?). *Chinese Dish, Rummer, Knife, Loaf of Bread and Fruit on a Table,* c. 1650-60. Oil on canvas, 44.7 x 38.8 cm.

18TH CENTURY PAINTING. FROM ROCOCO TO NEOCLASSICISM

ROOM 28

58. BOUCHER, François. *La Toilette,* 1742. Oil on canvas, 52.5 x 66.5 cm.

119. CHARDIN, Jean Baptiste Simeon. *Still-Life With Cat and Fish (Le Larron en Bonne Fortune),* 1728. Oil on canvas, 79.5 x 63 cm.

120. CHARDIN, Jean Baptiste Simeon. *Still-Life With Cat and Rayfish,* c. 1728. Oil on canvas, 79.5 x 63 cm.

148. FRAGONARD, Jean-Honoré. *The See-Saw (La Bascule).* Oil on canvas, 120 x 94.5 cm.

A 805. FRAGONARD, Jean-Honoré. *Portrait of a young lady (Mademoiselle Duthe?),* c. 1770. Oil on canvas, 53 cm. diam.

153. GAINSBOROUGH, Thomas. *Portrait of Miss Sarah Buxton,* 1776-1777. Oil on canvas, 110 x 87 cm.

215. LANCRET, Nicolas. *The Swing,* c. 1735-40. Oil on canvas, 65.5 x 54.5 cm.

216. LANCRET, Nicolas. *The Earth.* Oil on canvas, 38 x 31 cm.

217. LAWRENCE, Sir Thomas. *Portrait of David Lyon,* c. 1825. Oil on canvas, 217 x 132 cm.

219. LEPICIE, Nicolas-Bernard. *In the Courtyard of the Customs-House,* 1775. Oil on canvas, 98 x 164 cm.

A 818. LIOTARD. Jean-Etienne. *Portrait of a Woman in Maltese Costume.* Pastel on paper, 82.5 x 53.5 cm.

279. MAREES, George de. *Portrait of Maria Rosa Walburga von Soyer at Eisendorf,* 1750. Oil on canvas, 88 x 68 cm.

280. MAREES, George de. *Portrait of Franz Karl von Soyer at Eisendorf,* 1750. Oil on canvas, 88 x 68 cm.

297. NATTIER, Jean-Marc. *Portrait of Madame Bouret as Diana,* 1745. Oil on canvas, 138 x 105 cm.

313. PATER, Jean-Baptiste-Joseph. *Concert Champetre,* 1734. Oil on canvas, 53 x 68.5 cm.

334. REYNOLDS, Sir Joshua. *Portrait of Frances, Countess of Dartmouth,* 1757. Oil on canvas, 127 x 102 cm.

342. ROBERT, Hubert. *The Foot-Bridge,* c. 1775. Oil on canvas, 59 x 47 cm.

343. ROBERT, Hubert. *Interior of the Temple of Diana at Nimes,* 1783. Oil on canvas, 101 x 143 cm.

409. TROY, Jean François de. *Le Mariage de Jason.* Oil on canvas, 82 x 56 cm.

420. VERNET, Claude Joseph. *Marine, Tempete,* 1748. Oil on canvas, 44.5 x 60.5 cm.

421. VERNET, Claude Joseph. *Marine, Calme,* 1748. Oil on canvas, 44.5 x 60.5 cm.

431. WATTEAU, Jean Antoine. *The Rest,* c. 1709. Oil on canvas, 32 x 42.5 cm.

432. WATTEAU, Jean Antoine. *Pierrot Content,* c. 1712. Oil on canvas, 35 x 31 cm.

444. ZOFFANY, Johann. *Portrait of Miss Ann Brown in the Role of Miranda,* c. 1770. Oil on canvas, 218 x 158.5 cm.

445. ZOFFANY, Johann. *Group Portrait of Sir Elijah and Lady Impey,* 1783-1784. Oil on canvas, 91.5 x 122 cm.

NORTH AMERICAN PAINTING OF THE 19TH CENTURY

ROOM 29

A 884. BROWN, John George. *Tough Customers,* 1881. Oil on canvas, 76 x 63.5 cm.

A 885. CHASE, William Merritt. *Child Star Elsie Leslie Lyde as Little Lord Fauntleroy,* 1889. Oil on canvas, 176.2 x 100.3 cm.

507. CHURCH, Frederic Edwin. *Autumn,* 1875. Oil on canvas, 39 4 x 61 cm.

508. CHURCH, Frederic Edwin. *Cross in the Wilderness,* 1859. Oil on canvas, 41.3 x 61.5 cm.

509. CHURCH, Frederic Edwin. *Abandoned Skiff,* 1850. Oil on composition board, 28 x 43.2 cm.

91. CLONNEY, James Goodwyn. *Fishing Party on Long Island Sound Off New Rochelle,* 1847. Oil on canvas, 66 x 92.7 cm.

95. COLE, Thomas. *Expulsion. Moon and Firelight,* c. 1828. Oil on canvas, 91.4 x 122 cm.

96. COLE, Thomas. *Cross at Sunset,* c. 1848. Oil on canvas, 81.3 x 123.2 cm.

97. COPLEY, John Singleton. *Portrait of Mrs. Joshua Henshaw II (Catherine Hill),* c. 1772. Oil on canvas, 77 x 56 cm.

98. COPLEY, John Singleton. *Portrait of Mrs. Samuel Hill (Miriam Kilby),* c. 1764. Oil on canvas, 128.4 x 102 cm.

99. COPLEY, John Singleton. *Portrait of Judge Martin Howard,* 1767. Oil on canvas, 125.7 x 101 cm.

496. CROPSEY, Jasper Francis. *Greenwood Lake,* 1870. Oil on canvas, 97 x 174 cm.

533. DURAND, Asher Brown. *A Creek in the Woods,* 1865. Oil on canvas, 101.6 x 81.9 cm.

577. HEADE, Martin Johnson. *Spouting Rock, Newport,* 1862. Oil on canvas, 63.5 x 127 cm.

601. INNESS, George. *Summer Days,* 1857. Oil on canvas, 103.5 x 143 cm.

612. KENSETT, John Frederick. *Lake George,* c. 1860. Oil on canvas, 55.8 x 86.4 cm.

635. LANE, Fitz Hugh. *The Fort and Ten Pound Island, Gloucester, Massachusetts,* 1847. Oil on canvas, 50.8 x 76.2 cm.

315. PEALE, Charles Wilson. *Portrait of Isabella and John Stewart,* c. 1775. Oil on canvas, 94 x 124 cm.

364. SALMON, Robert. *View of Greenock, Scotland,* 1816. Oil on canvas, 66.6 x 112.3 cm.

A 867. SALMON, Robert. *Picture of the 'Dream' Pleasure Yacht,* 1839. Oil on panel, 42 X 62.5 cm.

760. SILVA, Francis A. *Kingston Point, Hudson River,* c. 1873. Oil on canvas, 51 x 91 cm.

383. STUART, Gilbert. *Presumed Portrait of George Washington Cook.* Oil on canvas, 76 x 63.5 cm.

ROOM 30

468. BIERSTADT, Albert. *Evening on the Prairie,* c. 1870. Oil on canvas, 81.3 x 123 cm.

A 832. BIERSTADT, Albert. *The Golden Gate,* 1900. Oil on canvas, 96.5 x 152.5 cm.

487. CATLIN, George. *The Falls of Saint Anthony,* 1871. Oil on board, 46 x 63.5 cm.

501. CHASE, William Merritt. *The Kimono,* c. 1895. Oil on canvas, 89.5 x 115 cm.

502. CHASE, William Merritt. *Shinnecock Hills,* 1893-1897. Oil on panel, 44.4 x 54.6 cm.

A 835. CHASE, William Merritt. *In the Park: A By-path,* 1890-1891. Oil on canvas, 35.5 x 49 cm.

574. HARNETT, William M.. *Materials for a Leisure Hour,* 1879. Oil on canvas, 38 x 51.5 cm.

588. HOMER, Winslow. *The Signal of Distress,* 1890. Oil on canvas, 62 x 98 cm.

589. HOMER, Winslow. *Waverly Oaks,* 1864. Oil on paper on panel, 33.6 x 25.4 cm.

591. HOMER, Winslow. *Portrait of Helena de Kay,* c. 1873. Oil on panel, 31 x 47 cm.

600. INNESS, George. *Morning,* c. 1878. Oil on canvas, 76.2 x 114.3 cm.

646. LEWIS, Henry. *Falls of Saint Anthony, Upper Mississippi,* 1847. Oil on canvas, 68.6 x 82.5 cm.

A 857. MORAN, Thomas. *Badlands of the Dakota,* 1901. Oil on canvas, 51 x 76 cm.

700. PETO, John Frederick. *Tom's River,* 1905. Oil on canvas, 50.8 x 40.6 cm.

701. PETO, John Frederick. *Afternoon Sailing,* c. 1890. Oil on canvas, 30.5 x 50.9 cm.

702. PETO, John Frederick. *Books, Mug, Pipe and Violin,* c. 1880. Oil on canvas, 63.5 x 50.9 cm.

722. REMINGTON, Frederic. *Apache Fire Signal,* c. 1908. Oil on canvas, 102 x 68.5 cm.

725. ROBINSON, Theodore. *The Old Bridge,* 1890. Oil on canvas, 63.5 x 81.2 cm.

731. SARGENT, John Singer. *Venetian Onion Seller,* c. 1880-1882. Oil on canvas, 95 x 70 cm.

732. SARGENT, John Singer. *Portrait of Millicent, Duchess of Sutherland,* 1904. Oil on canvas, 254 x 146 cm.

761. SLOAN, John. *Throbbing Fountain, Madison Square,* 1907. Oil on canvas, 66 x 81.5 cm.

784. WHISTLER, James Abbott McNeill. *Pink and Gold: The Neapolitan,* c. 1897. Oil on canvas, 50 x 31 cm.

785. WIMAR, Carl. *The Lost Trail,* c. 1856. Oil on canvas, 49.5 x 77.5 cm.

EUROPEAN PAINTING IN THE 19TH CENTURY. FROM ROMANTICISM TO REALISM

ROOM 31

470.a. BOECKLIN, Arnold. *A Nymph at the Fountain,* 1855. Pastel and coal on paper, 63 x 54 cm.

A 804. CONSTABLE, John R.A. *The Lock,* 1824. Oil on canvas, 142.2 x 120.7 cm.

494. COROT, Jean-Baptiste-Camile. *Setting Out for a Promenade in the Parc des Lions at Port-Marly,* c. 1872. Oil on canvas, 78 x 65 cm.

495. COURBET, Gustave. *The Water Stream, La Brème,* 1866. Oil on canvas, 114 x 89 cm.

A 836. COURBET, Gustave. *The Beach of Saint-Aubin-sur-Mer*, 1867. Oil on canvas, 54 x 65 cm.

126. DELACROIX, Eugene. *Arabian Rider*, c.1854. O l on canvas, 35 x 26.5 cm.

127. DELACROIX, Eugene. *The Duke of Orleans Revealing to the Duke of Burgundy His Lover*, c.1825-1826. Oil on canvas, 35 x 25.5 cm.

541. FANTIN-LATOUR, Henri. *Vase with Chrisanthemes*, 1875. Oil on canvas, 42.5 x 39.5 cm.

792. FRIEDRICH, Kaspar David. *Easter Morning*, 1833. Oil on canvas, 43.7 x 34.4 cm.

A 806. GAERTNER, Eduard. *View of the Opernplatz, the Opera and Unter den Linden, Berlin*, 1845. Oil on canvas, 42 x 78 cm.

157. GERICAULT, Theodore Jean Louis. *A Scene from the Free Horse Race*, 1816-1817. Oil on paper on canvas, 44 x 59 cm.

164. GOYA Y LUCIENTES, Francisco José de. *Portrait of King Ferdinand VII of Spain*, 1814-1815. Oil on canvas, 84 x 63.5 cm.

165. GOYA Y LUCIENTES, Francisco José de. *El Tio Paquete*, c. 1819-20. Oil on canvas, 39 x 31 cm.

166. GOYA Y LUCIENTES, Francisco José de. *Asensio Julia*, c. 1798. Oil on canvas, 54.5 x 41 cm.

A 844. GUILLAUMIN, Armand. *Still Life*, 1869. Oil on canvas, 50 x 61 cm.

177. HACKERT, Philipp Jacop. *View of the Palace at Caserta with the Vesuve*, 1793. Oil on canvas, 93 x 130 cm.

604. JONGKIND, Johann Barthold. *A View of the Harbour, Rotterdam*, 1856. Oil on canvas, 43 x 56 cm.

A 851. JONGKIND, Johann Barthold. *Landscape in Isère*, 1869. Oil on canvas, 41.5 x 65 cm.

205. KAUFFMANN, Angelica. *Portrait of a Young Lady as a Vestal Virgin*. Oil on canvas, 60 x 41 cm.

685. MOREAU, Gustave. *Galathea*, 1896. Oil and tempera on cardboard, 45 x 34 cm.

292. MORGENSTERN, Christian. *Trees on Water*, 1832. Oil on canvas, 71 x 100.5 cm.

429. WALDMUELLER, Ferdinand Georg. *Bad Ischl*, 1833. Oil on panel, 31.5 x 26.5 cm.

430. WALDMUELLER, Ferdinand Georg. *Der Schoenberg von der Hoisernradalpe*, 1833. Oil on panel, 31 x 25.7 cm.

IMPRESIONIST PAINTING
ROOM 32

476. BOUDIN, Eugène. *The Square of the Church of Saint Vulfran in Abbeville*, 1884. Oil on panel, 44.5 x 37 cm.

A 833. BOUDIN, Eugène. *Figures on the Beach at Trouville*, 1869. Oil on canvas, 29 x 47 cm.

A 834. BOUDIN, Eugène. *A Street in Abbeville with the Church of the Saint Vulfran*, 1894. Oil on panel, 44.5 x 37.5 cm.

A 845. GUILLAUMIN, Armand. *The Road to Damiette*, 1885. Oil on canvas, 65 x 81 cm.

659. MANET, Edouard. *Woman in Riding Habit, Fullface*, c. 1882. Oil on canvas, 73 x 52 cm.

680. MONET, Claude. *The Thaw at Vétheuil*, 1881. Oil on canvas, 60 x 100 cm.

A 856. MONET, Claude. *Cottage at Trouville: Low Tide*, 1881. Oil on canvas, 60 x 73.5 cm.

686. MORISOT, Berthe. *The Cheval-Glass*, 1876. Oil on canvas, 65 x 54 cm.

711. PISSARRO, Camille. *The Woods at Marly*, 1871. Oil on canvas, 45 x 55 cm.

712. PISSARRO, Camille. *Saint-Honoré Street in the Afternoon. Effect of Rain*, 1897. Oil on canvas, 81 x 65 cm.

A 861. PISSARRO, Camille. *Clearing at Eragny*, 1872. Oil on canvas, 74 x 92 cm.

724. RENOIR, Pierre-Auguste. *Woman with a Parasol in a Garden*, c. 1873. Oil on canvas. 54.5 x 65 cm.

A 864. RENOIR, Pierre-Auguste. *Young Girl Seated in an Interior*, 1879-1880. Pastel on paper, 61.5 x 46 cm.

A 865. RENOIR, Pierre-Auguste. *Cornfield*, 1879. Oil on canvas, 50.5 x 61 cm.

A 869. SISLEY, Alfred. *The Flood at Port-Marly*, 1876. Oil on canvas, 50 x 61 cm.

POSTIMPRESSIONIST PAINTING
ROOM 33

473. BONNARD, Pierre. *Portrait of Misia Godebska*, 1908. Oil on canvas, 145 x 114 cm.

488. CEZANNE, Paul. *Portrait of a Farmer*, 1901-1906. Oil on canvas, 65 x 54 cm.

515. DEGAS, Edgar. *Swaying Dancer (Dancer in Green)*, 1877-1879. Pastel on paper, 66 x 36 cm.

516. DEGAS, Edgar. *At the Milliner's*, c. 1883. Pastel on paper, 75.9 x 84.8 cm.

A 838. DEGAS, Edgar. *Race Horses: The Training,* 1894. Pastel on paper, 47.9 x 62.9 cm.

552. GAUGUIN, Paul. *Figure on the Road (Rouen),* 1884. Oil on canvas, 73 x 92 cm.

A 842. GAUGUIN, Paul. *Mata Mua (In Olden Times),* 1892. Oil on canvas, 91 x 69 cm.

557. GOGH, Vincent van. *The Stevedores in Arles,* 1888. Oil on canvas, 54 x 65 cm.

559. GOGH, Vincent van. *"Les Vessenots" in Auvers,* 1890. Oil on canvas, 55 x 65 cm.

788. GOGH, Vincent van. *Evening Landscape,* 1885. Oil on canvas laid down on board, 35 x 43 cm.

759. SICKERT, Walter Richard. *Giuseppina la Bague,* 1903-1904. Oil on canvas, 45.7 x 38.2 cm.

773. TOULOUSE-LAUTREC, Henri de. *Gaston Bonnefoy,* 1891. Oil on board, 71 x 37 cm.

774. TOULOUSE-LAUTREC, Henri de. *La Rousse in a White Blouse,* 1889. Oil on canvas, 59.5 x 48.2 cm.

FAUVE PAINTING
ROOM 34

524. DERAIN, André. *Waterloo Bridge,* 1906. Oil on canvas, 80.5 x 101 cm.

A 839. DUFY, Raoul. *Little Palm Tree,* 1905. Oil on canvas, 91 x 79 cm.

A 848. HODLER, Ferdinand. *Teenager in Bergbach,* 1901. Oil on canvas, 34 x 28 cm.

A 862. PRENDERGAST, Maurice. *Autumn,* 1910-1912. Oil on canvas, 49 x 62 cm.

A 887. PRENDERGAST, Maurice. *Still Life with Apples,* 1913 - 1915. Oil on canvas, 38 x 45.7 cm.

A 883. VLAMINCK, Maurice. *Olive-Trees,* 1905-1906. Oil on canvas, 53.5 x 65 cm.

EXPRESSIONIST PAINTING
ROOM 35

534. ENSOR, James. *Theatre of Masks,* 1908. Oil on canvas, 72 x 86 cm.

629. KOKOSCHKA, Oskar. *Portrait of Max Schmidt,* 1914. Oil on canvas, 90 x 57.5 cm.

664. MATISSE, Henri. *The Yellow Flowers,* 1902. Oil on canvas, 46 x 54.5 cm.

689. MUNCH, Edvard. *Evening,* 1888. Oil on canvas, 75 x 100.5 cm.

693. NOLDE, Emil. *Red Flowers,* 1906. Oil on canvas, 52.4 x 55.8 cm.

739. SCHIELE, Egon. *Houses on the River (The Old Town),* 1914. Oil on canvas, 100 x 120.5 cm.

ROOM 36

579. HECKEL, Erich. *Brickworks,* 1907. Oil on canvas, 68 x 86 cm.

A 847. HECKEL, Erich. *House in Dangast (The White House),* 1908. Oil on canvas, 71 x 81 cm.

A 853. KIRCHNER, Ernst Ludwig. *The Loam Pit,* c. 1906. Oil on board, 51 x 71 cm.

A 854.a. KIRCHNER, Ernst Ludwig. *Woman in front of Birch Trees,* c. 1907. Oil on canvas, 68.5 x 78 cm.

A 860. PECHSTEIN, Max. *Horse Fair,* 1910. Oil on canvas, 70 x 81 cm.

742. SCHMIDT-ROTTLUFF, Karl. *Autumn Landscape in Oldenburg,* 1907. Oil on canvas, 76 x 97.5 cm.

A 871. SCHMIDT-ROTTLUFF, Karl. *The little House,* 1906. Oil on board, 49.5 x 66.5 cm.

ROOM 37

613. KIRCHNER, Ernst Ludwig. *Doris with Ruff Collar,* c. 1906. Oil on board, 70.5 x 51 cm.

615.a. KIRCHNER, Ernst Ludwig. *Kneeling Nude in front of Red Screen,* c. 1911 - 1912. Oil on canvas, 75 x 56 cm.

616. KIRCHNER, Ernst Ludwig. *Alpine Kitchen,* 1918. Oil on canvas, 121.5 x 121.5 cm.

618. KIRCHNER, Ernst Ludwig. *Curving Bay,* 1914 (?). Oil on canvas, 146 x 123 cm.

789. KIRCHNER, Ernst Ludwig. *Fränzi in front of Carved Chair,* 1910. Oil on canvas, 71 x 49.5 cm.

687. MUELLER, Otto. *Two Female Nudes in a Landscape,* c. 1922 (?). Oil on burlap, 100 x 138 cm.

690. NOLDE, Emil. *Autumn Evening,* 1924. Oil on canvas, 73 x 100.5 cm.

691. NOLDE, Emil. *Summer Clouds,* 1913. Oil on canvas, 73.3 x 88.5 cm.

692. NOLDE, Emil. *Glowing Sunflowers,* 1936. Oil on canvas, 88.5 x 67.3 cm.

699. PECHSTEIN, Max. *Summer in Nidden,* 1919 or 1920. Oil on canvas, 81.3 x 101 cm.

A 870. SCHMIDT-ROTTLUFF, Karl. *Sun over Pine Forest,* 1913. Oil on canvas, 77 x 90.5 cm.

ROOM 38

485. BURLIUK, David. *Landscape,* 1912. Oil on canvas, 33 x 46.3 cm.

543. FEININGER, Lyonel. *Lady in Mauve,* 1922. Oil on canvas, 100.5 x 80.5 cm.

544. FEININGER, Lyonel. *Ships*, 1917. Oil on canvas, 71 x 85.5 cm.

545. FEININGER, Lyonel. *Architecture II (The Man from Potin)*, 1921. Oil on canvas, 101 X 80.5 cm.

A 840. FEININGER, Lyonel. *The White Man*, 1907. Oil on canvas, 68.3 x 52.3 cm.

602. ITTEN, Johannes. *Group of Houses in Spring*, 1916. Oil on canvas, 90 x 75 cm.

611. KANDINSKY, Wassily. *Murnau: Top of the Johannisstrasse*, 1908. Oil on board, 70 x 48.5

A 852. KANDINSKY, Wassily. *The Ludwigskirche in Munich*, 1908. Oil on board, 67.3 x 96 cm.

655. MACKE, August. *Hussars (Hussars on a Sortie)*, 1913. Oil on canvas, 37.5 x 56.1 cm.

656. MACKE, August. *Circus*, 1913. Oil on board, 47 x 63.5 cm.

660. MARC, Franz. *The Dream*, 1912. Oil on canvas, 100.5 x 135.5 cm.

688. MUENTER, Gabriele. *Self-portrait*, c. 1908. Oil on board, 49 x 33.6 cm.

ROOM 39

463. BECKMANN, Max. *Still life with yellow roses*, 1937. Oil on canvas, 110.5 x 65.5 cm.

464. BECKMANN, Max. *Quappi in pink jumper*, 1932-1935. Oil on canvas, 105 x 73 cm.

465. BECKMANN, Max. *Self-Portrait with raised hand*, 1908. Oil on canvas, 55 x 45 cm.

A 831. BECKMANN, Max. *Circus Artists*, 1948. Oil on canvas, 165 x 88.5 cm.

603. JAWLENSKY, Alexej von. *Red Veil*, 1912. Oil on board, 64.5 x 54 cm.

A 850. JAWLENSKY, Alexej von. *Child with Doll*, 1910. Oil on board, 61 x 50.5 cm.

637. LARIONOV, Michail. *The Baker*, 1909. Oil on canvas, 107 x 102 cm.

638. LARIONOV, Michail. *Blue Nude*, 1903. Oil on canvas, 73 x 116 cm.

ROOM 40

525. DIX, Otto. *Hugo Erfurth With a Dog*, 1926. Tempera and oil on plywood panel, 80 x 100 cm.

569. GROSZ, George. *Metropolis (View of the Metropolis)*, 1916 - 1617. Oil on canvas, 100 x 102 cm.

572. GROSZ, George. *Street Scene (Kurfürstendamm)*, 1925. Oil on canvas, 81.3 x 61.3 cm.

582. HENRICH, Albert. *Portrait of the Painter A. M. Tränkler*, 1926. Oil on canvas, 81 x 62 cm.

596. HUBBUCH, Karl. *Twice Hilde II*, c. 1929. Oil on canvas mounted on board, 150 x 77 cm.

614. KIRCHNER. Ernst Ludwig. *With Red Streetwalker*, 1914-1925. Oil on canvas, 125 x 90.5 cm.

671. MEIDNER, Ludwig. *The Corner House (Villa Kochmann, Dresden)*, 1913. Oil on canvas on board, 97.2 x 78 cm.

733. SCHAD, Christian. *Portrait of Dr. Haustein*, 1928. Oil on canvas, 80.5 x 55 cm.

734. SCHAD, Christian. *Maria and Annunziata 'from the Harbour'*, 1923. Oil on canvas, 67.5 x 55.5 cm.

741. SCHLICHTER, Rudolf. *Portrait of an Oriental Journalist*, c. 1923-1924. Oil on canvas, 73.5 x 50.5 cm.

RESTING AREA

A 872. TOULOUSE-LAUTREC, Henri de. *At the Moulin Rouge: The Goulou and Môme Fromage*, 1892. Color lithograph, 45.5 x 34.7 cm.

A 873. TOULOUSE-LAUTREC, Henri de. *The Englishman at the Moulin Rouge*, 1892. Color lithograph, 52.5 x 37.2 cm.

A 874. TOULOUSE-LAUTREC, Henri de. *The Jockey*, 1899. Color lithograph, 51.5 x 36.2 cm.

A 875. TOULOUSE-LAUTREC, Henri de. *Mademoiselle Marcelle Lender standing*, 1895. Color lithograph, 36 x 24.7 cm.

A 876. TOULOUSE-LAUTREC, Henri de. *The Sitting Clowness: Mlle. Chau-u-kao*, 1896. Color lithograph, 52 x 40.5 cm.

A 877. TOULOUSE-LAUTREC, Henri de. *The Clowness at the Moulin Rouge: Mlle. Chau-u-Kao*, 1897. Color lithograph, 41.2 x 32.3 cm.

A 878. TOULOUSE-LAUTREC, Henri de. *The Dance at the Moulin Rouge*, 1897. Color lithograph, 45.5 x 36 cm.

A 879. TOULOUSE-LAUTREC, Henri de. *The Large Box*, 1897. Color lithograph, 51 x 41 cm.

A 880. TOULOUSE-LAUTREC, Henri de. *The Englishman at the Moulin Rouge*, 1892. Color lithograph, 48 x 37.8 cm.

A 881. TOULOUSE-LAUTREC, Henri de. *Elsa the Viennese*, 1897. Color lithograph, 58 x 39.5 cm.

EXPERIMENTAL AVANT-GARDES

ROOM 41

459. BALLA, Giacomo. *Patriotic Demonstration*, 1915. Tempera on canvas, 100 x 136.5 cm.

517. DELAUNAY, Robert. *Woman with a Parasol. (The Parisian)*, 1913. Oil on canvas, 122 x 85.5 cm.

518. DELAUNAY-TERK, Sonia. *Simultaneous Contrasts*, 1913. Oil on canvas, 55 x 46 cm.

519. DELAUNAY-TERK, Sonia. *Simultaneous Robes. (The Three Women)*, 1925. Oil on canvas, 146 x 114 cm.

526. DOESBURG, Theo van. *Still Even Composition*, 1916. Oil on canvas, 45 x 32 cm.

540. EXTER, Alexandra. *Still Life with Bottle and Glass*, 1912. Collage and oil on canvas, 68 x 53 cm.

555. GLEIZES, Albert. *At the Harbour*, 1917. Oil and sand on wood, 153 x 120 cm.

562. GONTCHAROVA, Natalia. *Rayonist Landscape (La Forêt)*, 1913. Oil on canvas, 130 x 97 cm.

583. HERBIN, Auguste. *Cubist Composition*, 1918. Oil on canvas, 60 x 37.5 cm.

633. KUPKA, Frantisek. *The Machine Drill*, 1925. Oil on canvas, 73 x 85 cm.

634. KUPKA, Frantisek. *Localization of Graphic Mobiles*, 1912-1913. Oil on canvas, 200 x 194 cm.

790. KUPKA, Frantisek. *Study for the Language of Verticals*, 1911. Oil on canvas, 78 x 63 cm.

636. LARIONOV, Michail. *Street with Lanterns*, 1910. Oil on burlap, 35 x 50 cm.

639. LARIONOV, Michail. *Still Life with Carafe and Curtains*, c. 1914. Oil on canvas, 41 x 29 cm.

715. POPOVA, Liubov. *Still Life. Instruments*, 1915. Oil on canvas, 105.5 x 69.2 cm.

730. ROZANOVA, Olga. *Man on the Street (Analysis of Volumes)*, 1913. Oil on canvas, 83 x 61.5 cm.

752. SEVERINI, Gino. *Expansion of Light*, 1912. Oil on canvas, 68.5 x 43.2 cm.

776. UDALZOVA, Nadeshda. *Cubism*, 1914. Oil on canvas, 72 x 60 cm.

ROOM 42

453. ANNENKOV, Yuri. *Amiens Cathedral*, 1919. Collage, wood, cardboard, and wire on paper, 71 x 52 cm.

481. BRUCE, Patrick Henry. *Painting. Still Life*, c. 1923-1924. Oil and pencil on canvas, 63.5 x 81.3 cm.

575. HARTLEY, Marsden. *Musical Theme No. 2 (Bach Preludes et Fugues)*, 1912. Oil on canvas mounted on masonite, 61 x 50.8 cm.

642. LECK, Bart van der. *Woodhacker*, 1927. Oil on canvas, 70.5 x 59 cm.

780. WADSWORTH, Edward. *Vorticist Abstraction*, 1915. Oil on canvas, 76.3 x 63.5 cm.

782. WEBER, Max. *Grand Central Terminal*, 1915. Oil on canvas, 152.5 x 101.6 cm.

ROOM 43

506. CHASHNIK, Ilya. *Suprematist Composition*, 1923. Oil on canvas, 183.5 x 112 cm.

528. DOESBURG, Theo van. *Composition*, 1919 - 1920. Oil on canvas, 92 x 71 cm.

599. HUSZAR, Vilmos. *Composition*, 1920-1922. Oil on board, 84.2 x 61.4 cm.

625. KLIUN, Ivan Wasilewitsch. *Composition*, 1917. Oil on canvas, 88 x 69 cm.

641. LECK, Bart van der. *Algerian Landscape with a Hamlet*, 1917. Gouache on parchment paper, 100 x 154 cm.

651. LISSITZKY, Eliezer. *Proun 4 B*, 1919-1920. Oil on canvas, 70 x 55.5 cm.

652. LISSITZKY, Eliezer. Proun 1 C, 1919. Oil on plywood, 68 x 68 cm.

675. MOHOLY-NAGY, Laszló. *Large Railway Painting*, 1920. Oil on canvas, 100 x 77 cm.

676. MOHOLY-NAGY, Laszló. *Circle Segments*, 1921. Tempera on canvas, 78 x 60 cm.

677. MONDRIAN, Piet. *Composition I*, 1931. Oil on canvas, 50 x 50 cm.

679. MONDRIAN, Piet. *New York City, New York*, c. 1942. Oil, pencil, charcoal and painted tape on canvas, 117 x 110 cm.

714. POPOVA, Liubov. *Pictorial Architectonic*, 1918. Oil on canvas, 45 x 53 cm.

716. POPOVA, Liubov. *Architectonic Composition*, c. 1917. Oil on burlap, 70.5 x 70.5 cm.

745. SCHWITTERS, Kurt. *Picture From 8 Sides*, 1930. Oil on panel, 91 x 90 cm.

746. SCHWITTERS, Kurt. *Merzbild 1A (The Psychiatrist)*, 1919. Mixed media, montage on canvas, 48.5 x 38.5 cm.

747. SCHWITTERS, Kurt. *Merzbild Kijkduin*, 1923. Mixed media on board, 74.3 x 60.3 cm.

748. SCHWITTERS, Kurt. *Merz 1925, 1. Relief in the Blue Square*, 1925. Mixed media on board, 49.5 x 50.2 cm.

767. SUETIN, Nikolai. *Suprematismus,* 1920 - 1921. Oil on canvas, 53 x 70.5 cm.

778. VORDEMBERGE-GILDEWART, Friedrich. *Composition N. 104, White on White,* 1936. Oil on canvas, 60 x 60 cm

ROOM 44

478. BRAQUE, Georges. *Woman with a Mandolin,* 1910. Oil on canvas, 80.5 x 54 cm.

479. BRAQUE, Georges. *Le Parc de Carrières-Saint-Denis,* 1908 - 1909. Oil on canvas, 40.6 x 45.3 cm.

565. GRIS, Juan. *Still Life,* 1911. Charcoal on silkpaper, 74 x 43 cm.

566. GRIS, Juan. *Bottle and Fruit-Dish,* 1919. Oil on canvas, 74 x 54 cm.

567. GRIS, Juan. *The Smoker,* 1913. Oil on canvas, 73 x 54 cm.

A 843. GRIS, Juan. *Sitting woman,* 1917. Oil on panel, 116 x 73 cm.

645. LEGER, Fernand. *The Staircase (Second State),* 1914. Oil on canvas, 88 x 124.5 cm.

678. MONDRIAN, Piet. *Grey-Blue Composition,* 1912-1913. Oil on canvas, 79.5 x 63.5 cm.

705. PICASSO, Pablo Ruiz. *Head,* c. 1906 - 1907. Gouache on brown paper, 31 x 24.5 cm.

707. PICASSO, Pablo Ruiz. *Head of a Man,* 1913-1914. Oil on canvas, 65 x 46 cm.

708. PICASSO, Pablo Ruiz. *Still Life: Glasses and Fruit,* 1908. Oil on canvas, 27 x 21.6 cm.

710. PICASSO, Pablo Ruiz. *Man with a Clarinette,* 1911 - 1912. Oil on canvas, 106 x 69 cm.

THE SYNTHESIS OF MODERNISM IN EUROPE

ROOM 45

480. BRAQUE, Georges. *The Pink Tablecloth,* 1938. Oil and sand on canvas, 87.5 x 106 cm.

497. CHAGALL, Marc. *The Madonna of the Village,* 1938-1942. Oil on canvas, 102.5 x 98 cm.

499. CHAGALL, Marc. *The Rooster,* 1929. Oil on canvas, 81 x 65.5 cm.

500. CHAGALL, Marc. *The House in Grey,* 1917. Oil on canvas, 68 x 74 cm.

537. ERNST, Max. *33 Girls pursuing a White Butterfly,* 1958. Oil on canvas, 137 x 107 cm.

538. ERNST, Max. *Untitled (Dada),* c. 1922. Oil on canvas, 43.2 x 31.5 cm.

547. FONTANA, Lucio. *The Gold of Venice,* 1961. Acrylic on canvas, 149 x 149 cm. *Exhibited in Main Hall

606. KANDINSKY, Wassily. *Around the Line,* 1943. Oil on board, 42 x 57.8 cm.

608. KANDINSKY, Wassily. *In the Bright Oval,* 1925. Oil on board, 73 x 59 cm.

609. KANDINSKY, Wassily. *Picture with Three Spots,* 1914. Oil on canvas, 121 x 111 cm.

623. KLEE, Paul. *Omega 5 (295) 'Dummy',* 1927. Oil and watercolor on canvas stuck down on board, 57.3 x 43 cm.

624. KLEE, Paul. *Revolving House,* 1921. Oil+gouache on primed cheesecloth stuck down on watercolor paper, 37.7 x 52.2 cm.

643. LEGER, Fernand. *Composition. The Disc,* 1918. Oil on canvas, 65 x 54 cm.

644. LEGER, Fernand. *The Terrace,* 1922. Gouache on paper, 23 x 31 cm.

A 855. LEGER, Fernand. *The Bridge,* 1923. Oil on canvas, 92 x 60 cm.

672. MIRO, Joan. *Catalan Peasant with a Guitar,* 1924. Oil on canvas, 148 x 114 cm.

673. MIRO, Joan. *Painting on White Ground,* 1927. Oil on canvas, 55 x 46 cm.

674. MIRO, Joan. *The Lightning Bird Blinded by Moonfire,* 1955. Oil on cardboard, 25 x 20 cm.

A 836. MIRO, Joan. *Composition 1926,* 1926. Oil on canvas, 72.5 x 92 cm.

706. PICASSO, Pablo Ruiz. *Bullfight,* 1934. Oil on canvas, 54 x 73 cm.

709. PICASSO, Pablo Ruiz. *Harlequin with a Mirror,* 1923. Oil on canvas, 100 x 81 cm.

764. STAEL, Nicolas de. *Grey Composition,* 1948. Oil on canvas, 150 x 75 cm.

SCULPTURES

S 58. GIACOMETTI, Alberto *The Glade,* 1950. Bronze with brown patina, Height:59.5 cm.

S 59. MOORE, Henry. *Reclining Figure No. 4,* 1954. Bronze with dark patina, Height: 58.5 cm.

THE SYNTHESIS OF MODERNISM IN THE U.S.A.

ROOM 46

450. ALBERS, José. *Casablanca B,* 1947-1954. Oil on cardboard, 41.3 x 60.7 cm.

563. GORKY, Arshile. *Hugging/ (Good Hope Road II)/ (Pastoral),* 1945. Oil on canvas, 64.7 x 82.7 cm.

564. GORKY, Arshile. *Last Painting (The Black Monk),* 1948. Oil on canvas, 78.6 x 101.5 cm.

587. HOFMANN, Hans. *Untitled (Renate series),* 1965. Oil on canvas, 121.9 x 91.4 cm.

630. KOONING, Willem de. *Abstraction,* 1949-1950. Mixed media on fiberboard, 37 x 46.5 cm.

631. KOONING, Willem de. *Red Man with Moustache,* 1971. Oil on paper mounted on canvas, 186 x 91.5 cm.

653. LOUIS, Morris. *Pillars of Hercules,* 1960. Acrylic on canvas, 231.1 x 267.3 cm.

670. MATTA, Roberto. *Composition,* 1939. Oil on canvas, 30.5 x 40.5 cm.

695. O'KEEFFE, Georgia. *Abstraction,* 1920. Oil on canvas, 71 x 61 cm.

697. O'KEEFFE, Georgia. *White Iris No. 7,* 1957. Oil on canvas, 76.2 x 102 cm.

A 859. O'KEEFFE, Georgia. *New York with Moon,* 1925. Oil on canvas, 122 x 77 cm.

713. POLLOCK, Jackson. *Brown and Silver I,* c. 1951. Enamel and silver paint on canvas, 145 x 101 cm.

729. ROTHKO, Mark. *Green on Maroon,* 1961. Mixed media on canvas, 258 x 229 cm.

765. STELLA, Frank. *Untitled,* 1966. Alkyd on canvas, 91.5 x 91.5 cm. *Exhibited in Main Hall

766. STILL, Clyfford. *Untitled,* 1965. Oil on canvas, 254 x 176.5 cm.

771. TOBEY, Mark. *Earth Rhythm,* 1961. Gouache on board, 67 x 49 cm.

SURREALISM. FIGURATIVE TRADITION AND POP ART

ROOM 47

455. AUERBACH, Frank. *Head of J. Y. M.,* 1978. Oil on canvas, 61 x 66 cm.

460. BALTHUS. *The Card Game,* 1948-1950. Oil on canvas, 140 x 194 cm.

A 837. CRAWFORD, Ralston. *Overseas Highway,* 1939. Oil on canvas, 45.7 x 76.2 cm.

510. DALÍ, Salvador. *Dream caused by the Flight of a Bee Around a Promegranate a Second before Awakening,* 1944 Oil on panel, 51 x 41 cm.

511. DALÍ, Salvador. *Gradiva Discovers the Ruins of Antropomorphos,* 1931. Oil on canvas, 65 x 54 cm.

520. DELVAUX, Paul. *Woman in the Mirror,* 1936. Oil on canvas, 71 x 91.5 cm.

535. ERNST, Max. *Solitary and Conjugal Trees,* 1940. Oil on canvas, 81.5 x 100.5 cm.

546. FILONOV, Pavel Nikolaevitch. *Untitled,* 1927. Oil on canvas, 236.5 x 153 cm.

551. FREUD, Lucian. *Portrait of Baron H. H. Thyssen-Bornemisza,* 1981-1982. Oil on canvas, 51 x 40 cm.

554. GIACOMETTI, Alberto. *Portrait of a Woman,* 1965. Oil on canvas, 86 x 65 cm.

594. HOPPER, Edward. *Hotel Room,* 1931. Oil on canvas, 152.4 x 165.7 cm.

595. HOPPER, Edward. *Girl at a Sewing Machine,* 1921-1922. Oil on canvas, 48.3 x 46 cm.

A 849. HOPPER, Edward. *The Martha McKeen of Wellfleet,* 1944. Oil on canvas, 81.5 x 127.5 cm.

632. KOSSOFF, Leon. *Booking Hall, Kilburn Underground Station No. 1,* 1976. Oil on board, 45.7 x 38.1 cm.

657. MAGRITTE, René. *The Key to the Fields,* 1936. Oil on canvas, 80 x 60 cm.

754. SHAHN, Ben. *Four Piece Orchestra,* 1944. Tempera on masonite, 45.7 x 60.1 cm.

756. SHAHN, Ben. *Carnival,* 1946. Tempera on masonite, 56 x 75.5 cm.

757. SHEELER, Charles. *Canyons,* 1951. Oil on canvas, 63.5 x 56 cm.

768. TANGUY, Yves. *Imaginary Numbers,* 1954. Oil on canvas, 99 x 80 cm.

769. TANGUY, Yves. *Composition (Mort guettant sa famille),* 1927. Oil on canvas, 100 x 73 cm.

770. TANGUY, Yves. *Still and Always,* 1942. Oil on canvas, 100 x 81 cm.

787. WYETH, Andrew. *My Young Friend,* 1970. Tempera on masonite, 81.3 x 63.5 cm.

ROOM 48

451. ANDREWS, Michael. *Portrait of Timothy Behrens,* 1962. Oil on hardboard, 122 x 122 cm.

458. BACON, Francis. *Portrait of George Dyer in a Mirror,* 1968. Oil on canvas, 198 x 147 cm.

491. CORNELL, Joseph. *Juan Gris Cockatoo Nº 4,* c. 1953-1954. Construction, 50 x 30 x 11.5 cm.

492. CORNELL, Joseph. *Blue Soap Bubble,* 1949-1950. Construction, 24.5 x 30.5 x 9.6 cm.

513. DAVIS, Stuart. *Sweet Caporal,* 1922. Oil and watercolor on canvas board, 51 x 47 cm.

514. DAVIS, Stuart. *Pochade,* 1958. Oil on canvas, 130 x 152 cm.

521. DEMUTH, Charles. *Love, Love, Love. Homage to Gertrude Stein,* 1928. Oil on panel, 51 x 53 cm.

539. ESTES, Richard. *Telephone Booths,* 1967. Acrylic on masonite, 122 x 175.3 cm.

549. FREUD, Lucian. *Large Interior, Paddington,* 1968-1969. Oil on canvas, 183 x 122 cm.

550. FREUD, Lucian. *Reflection with Two Children (Self Portrait),* 1965. Oil on canvas, 91 x 91 cm.

584. HOCKNEY, David. I*n Memoriam of Cecchino Bracci,* 1962. Oil on canvas, 213.3 x 91.4 cm.

619. KITAJ, Ronald B. *Smyrna Greek (Nicos),* 1976 - 1977. Oil on canvas, 243.8 x 76.2 cm.

620. KITAJ, Ronald B. *A Visit to London (Robert Creeley and Robert Duncan),* 1977. Oil on canvas, 182.9 x 61 cm.

648. LICHTENSTEIN, Roy. *A Woman in Bath,* 1963. Oil on canvas, 171 x 171 cm.

649. LINDNER, Richard. *Moon over Alabama,* 1963. Oil on canvas, 202 x 102 cm.

721. RAUSCHENBERG, Robert. *Express,* 1963. Oil on canvas with silkscreen, 183 x 305 cm.

728. ROSENQUIST, James. *Smoked Glass,* 1962. Oil on canvas, 61 x 81.5 cm.

783. WESSELMANN, Tom. *Nude N. 1,* 1970. Oil on canvas, 63.5 x 114.5 cm.

STAIRS

486. BURLIUK, Vladimir. *Russian Peasant Woman,* 1910-1911. Oil on canvas, 132 x 70 cm.

490. CORINTH, Lovis. *Fashion Show,* 1921. Oil on canvas, 201.5 x 100 cm.

523. DEPERO, Fortunato. *Robot. Mechanical Composition,* 1920. Mixed media, 67.5 x 52.5 cm.

146. FOSCHI, Francesco. *Winter Landscape in the Apennines.* Oil on canvas, 48 x 62 cm.

147. FOSCHI, Francesco. *Winter Landscape in the Apennines.* Oil on canvas, 48 x 62 cm.

556. GNOLI, Domenico. *Armchair,* 1967. Oil and salt on canvas, 203 x 143 cm.

173. GRIMALDI, Giovanni Francesco (Detto BOLGNESE). *Landscape with Tobias and the Angel,* after 1630. Oil on canvas, 174 x 126 cm.

A 846.a. HECKEL, Erich. *Female Head (Portrait of Sidor Heckel),* 1913. Oil on canvas, 70 x 60 cm.

617. KIRCHNER, Ernst Ludwig. *The Junkerboden under Snow.* Oil on canvas, 100 x 120 cm.

338. RICCI, Marco. *Winter Landscape.* Oil on canvas, 173 x 232 x 4 cm.

367. SCHOENFELD, Heinrich. *Salomon and the Queen of Sheba.* Oil on canvas, 82 x 112 cm.

SCULPTURES

S 53. *Saint Jerome in penitence,* CANO, Alonso (by a follower of). Terracotta, painted, Height: 43.5 cm

CAFETERIA AND AUDITORIUM AREA

452. ANDREWS, Michael. *Lights V: The Pier Pavilion,* 1973. Acrylic on canvas, 152.4 x 213.3 cm.

573. GUTTUSO, Renato. *Caffè Greco,* 1976. Acrylic on carton over canvas, 186 x 243 cm.

665. MATTA, Roberto. *Great Expectations. From the Cycle:"The Blinding Exile",* 1966. Oil on canvas, 203 x 402 cm.

666. MATTA, Roberto. *Where Madness Dwells A. From the Cycle:"The Blinding Exile",* 1966. Oil on canvas, 205 x 203.5 cm.

667. MATTA, Roberto. *The Blinding Exile. From the Cycle:"The Blinding Exile",* 1966. Oil on canvas, 200 x 195 cm.

668. MATTA, Roberto. *The Where at Flood Tide. From the Cycle:"The Blinding Exile",* 1966 Oil on canvas, 202 x 195 cm.

669. MATTA, Roberto. *Where Madness Dwells B. From the Cycle:"The Blinding Exile".* 1966. Oil on canvas, 204 x 204.5 cm.

LUNWERG EDITORES S.A.
General Manager: *Juan Carlos Luna*
Art Director: *Andrés Gamboa*
Technical Director: *Santiago Carregal*
Layout: *Alberto Caffaratto*

FUNDACIÓN COLECCIÓN THYSSEN-BORNEMISZA
Publishing coordinator: *Alicia Martínez Vélez*

Photographs
José Loren
Joaquín Cortés
Villa Favorita

Collaboration
Hans Hoetink

Translated by
Charles Dietz